"Fr. James Heft has created a much needed and important scholarly research center with the IACS. . . . It provides some brilliant insights into the state of the field and makes the case why the work of the IACS is so very necessary, not only for academia, but for the world which we all share."
—AMIR HUSSAIN, past president, American Academy of Religion, and professor of theological studies, Loyola Marymount University

"Intellectual and institutional histories benefit from both broad overviews and detailed studies. Jim Heft's engaging narrative of his struggles and successes in developing the Institute for Advanced Catholic Studies offers readers the kind of local history that adds texture to our broader understanding of the intellectual sweep of American Catholicism and the complex diversity of American higher education."
—MARK W. ROCHE, Rev. Edmund P. Joyce, CSC, Professor of German Language and Literature and Concurrent Professor of Philosophy, University of Notre Dame

"Beyond the history of a Catholic research institute, Heft offers a lively personal take on trends in the Catholic intellectual world from the 1930s to the 2020s—including bishops, universities, scholars, funders, the Catholic 'culture wars,' and the impact of Pope Francis. . . . This book recreates a vivid journey back to twentieth-century political dynamics around Catholic theology, especially worries about its genuine 'Catholicity.' Heft writes with the authority and investment of a survivor!"
—LISA SOWLE CAHILL, J. Donald Monan, SJ, Professor of Theology, Boston College

"The world's ideas matter greatly, and an institute that attempts to consider the world's most pressing questions in the context of our highest ideals and beliefs is a true gift. Heft and his early collaborators have done exactly that in creating the Institute for Advanced Catholic Studies at USC. The IACS was the result of sheer will, resistance to those who pushed back, and the success that comes from bringing some of the world's finest minds to bear on questions that matter."
—DENNIS HOLTSCHNEIDER, CM, president emeritus, Association of Catholic Colleges and Universities, and Joseph Cardinal Bernardin Fellow of Church Leadership, Catholic Theological Union, Chicago

"I know Father Dr. Professor James L. Heft, SM, as Jim, and he knows me as Reuven. I have had the enormous pleasure of learning from him, co-teaching with him, sharing podia with him, and sitting alongside him in classrooms, boardrooms, and lecture halls. As I look back at my own spiritual and academic career as a practicing Jew, a rabbi, and an academic, I don't think I ever had more stimulating growth experiences than I was afforded as Jim's colleague and fellow traveler in the quest for combining academic and spiritual excellence through the IACS. Jim's energy, kindness, honesty, and humility are matched only by his intellectual integrity and willingness to honestly consider virtually any question from virtually any angle."
—REUVEN FIRESTONE, Regenstein Professor in Medieval Judaism and Islam, Hebrew Union College, and affiliate professor, University of Southern California

"This 'personal history' of the Institute for Advanced Catholic Studies at the University of Southern California is an absorbing, frank account of an important—and ongoing—contribution to US Catholic intellectual life. More than a memoir or a chronicle, it is a compelling vision of the gifts that scholars bring to the church and the world, and the challenges involved in providing time and space for those gifts to flourish. Current workers in this particular vineyard, as well as future historians, will find information and inspiration here."

—UNA CADEGAN, professor of history, University of Dayton

The Institute for Advanced Catholic Studies
at the University of Southern California

# The Institute for Advanced Catholic Studies
## at the University of Southern California

A Personal History

JAMES L. HEFT, SM
*Foreword by Cardinal Robert W. McElroy*

WIPF & STOCK · Eugene, Oregon

THE INSTITUTE FOR ADVANCED CATHOLIC STUDIES AT THE
UNIVERSITY OF SOUTHERN CALIFORNIA
A Personal History

Copyright © 2025 James L. Heft, SM. All rights reserved. Except for brief quotations in critical publications or reviews, no part of this book may be reproduced in any manner without prior written permission from the publisher. Write: Permissions, Wipf and Stock Publishers, 199 W. 8th Ave., Suite 3, Eugene, OR 97401.

Wipf & Stock
An Imprint of Wipf and Stock Publishers
199 W. 8th Ave., Suite 3
Eugene, OR 97401

www.wipfandstock.com

PAPERBACK ISBN: 979-8-3852-3246-8
HARDCOVER ISBN: 979-8-3852-3247-5
EBOOK ISBN: 979-8-3852-3248-2

VERSION NUMBER 010925

In appreciation of all those who, despite opposition,
dedicated the time, financial support, and leadership to build
this unique intellectual resource for Catholic education,
the Church, and the world.

# Contents

*Foreword by Cardinal Robert W. McElroy* | ix
*Preface* | xiii
*Acknowledgments* | xv
*Introduction: A Seed Planted* | xix

1. Research Institutes—Secular and Catholic | 1
2. Collaborating to Build a New Institution | 15
3. Establishing a Board of Trustees and an Academic Advisory Council | 32
4. Competition or Complementarity? | 40
5. Criticism and Controversy | 46
6. Conflict with Another Cardinal | 52
7. Fundraising and Foundation Pledge Agreement | 59
8. Do We Persevere or Close Up Shop? | 65
9. Going Full Time: Go West! | 77
10. Capital Campaign and Communicating the Mission | 86
11. On a Roll—People and Programs (2015–2020) | 99
12. Stepping Down as President | 105

APPENDICES

Appendix A: Prospectus: Institute for Advanced Catholic Studies | 109
Appendix B: Commission on Catholic Scholarship | 110
Appendix C: Board of Trustees and Academic Advisory Council | 111

Appendix D: The Need and The Benefits | 112

Appendix E: John T. Noonan Jr. *America* Article | 113

Appendix F: Correspondence with Archbishop Pilarczyk Re: Cardinal Ratzinger | 114

Appendix G: IACS Book Offerings | 118

Appendix H: Generations in Dialogue Program | 119

Appendix I: Endowed Fellowships | 120

Appendix J: Elevator Speech | 121

Appendix K: World Religions: Finding Common Ground Program | 123

Appendix L: Youth, the Catholic Church, and Our Future | 124

Appendix M: 2017 IACS Board of Trustees | 125

Appendix N: 2023 IACS Board of Trustees | 126

*Works Cited* | 127
*Index* | 131

# Foreword

FATHER JIM HEFT DESCRIBES his new book on the establishment of the Institute for Advanced Catholic Studies at the University of Southern California as a personal journal and narrative. And on one level it is, for it describes the exhilarating and often challenging journey that Heft undertook in the 1990s to found a research and resource center that could systematically highlight for faculty, especially at Catholic universities, the integrating and enriching lens that Catholicism brings to a wide variety of academic disciplines. Through deep vision, rugged persistence, and the collaboration of talented lay and clerical leaders dedicated to the urgency of renewing the Catholic intellectual tradition as an integrating force, the Institute's founders surmounted obstacles of bureaucracy, finance, canon law, rejection, dejection, and interpersonal conflicts. Critically, they were fortunate to find an incredibly welcoming and supportive home for their project at the University of Southern California, where the Institute has become a leaven within Catholic university life in the United States and beyond.

Engaging as Heft's narrative journey is, it decidedly is not confined to the specific history of the Institute for Advanced Catholic Studies itself, but points to major currents, tensions, and opportunities in Catholic higher education in the United States.

The first of these is the decline in strength of the Catholic intellectual tradition in the faculties of Catholic universities, even amidst the rise in the level of general academic quality on so many Catholic campuses in our country. Heft points to the enduring need to create and deepen a Catholic imagination within the teaching and administrative leadership of Catholic universities, an imagination proceeding from the Incarnation and the Pascal Mystery that lie at the center of Catholic faith.

A second major element that shaped and often impeded Heft's project is what he terms "localism" within Catholic university communities—the tendency to myopically evaluate opportunities for deep collaboration among Catholic universities within a framework that values the wellbeing of the unitary college or university rather than comprehensively within the constellation of Catholic institutions of higher learning. Localism is an understandable perspective in Catholic university life, but it can be a terrible corrosion of the fundamental notion of our faith that all should be one.

The history of the Institute is replete with the interventions of bishops who saw great vision and great faith in the effort to establish a national institute for nourishing the Catholic intellectual tradition among members of Catholic university faculties. But it also bears the imprint of episcopal actions rooted in fear of the loss of control and a continuing discomfort with the level of legitimate autonomy that is necessary for effective Catholic higher education in the United States. This persistent tension between bishops and universities, which was so prominent during the divides over *Ex Corde Ecclesiae* and has now settled in an all-too-common relationship of benign neglect on both sides, has impeded substantive progress on the key themes of mission, freedom, and fidelity as they are emerging in the present day.

Finally, Father Heft's book concludes with a reflection on the distinctive prophetic lens which Pope Francis has brought to the Church's own self-understanding of the nature of theology and academic mission. Signaling a conversion within his own thinking after wrestling with this question for most of his life, Heft notes that "the value of the Catholic intellectual tradition, therefore, is not only a matter of understanding, of Logos. It is also a matter of witness and deeds of justice, of *praxis*" (p. 97). This conversion lies at the center of every effort to point to the integrating legacy that the Catholic intellectual tradition must seek within the broad life of the university in this new millennium, and it points to the renewal of theology that Pope Francis's *motu proprio Theologiam Promovendam* framed in 2023. Thus, it is a fitting testimony to the fact that the mission of the Institute for Advanced Catholic Studies remains as necessary today as it was in the years after World War II when it was originally envisioned.

Cardinal Robert W. McElroy<br>December 5, 2024

# Preface

FROM 1845 TO 1924, Catholic immigrants came in waves to the United States. The Protestants who dominated the country's culture and government feared that Catholics would weaken their hard-won democracy and religious freedom. In this hostile environment, Catholic immigrants, led by their bishops and supported by many religious orders, especially of women, proceeded to build the largest primary and secondary educational system in the world. Today, US Catholics, who comprise 6 percent of the world's Catholics, have established nearly 20 percent of all Catholic colleges and universities in the world, some of them internationally recognized.

The post–Vatican II (1962–1965) period witnessed a massive exodus of members of religious orders responsible for establishing 90 percent of these educational institutions. Lay faculty, many with impressive degrees from secular institutions, hold the vast majority of faculty positions and presidencies. Many have little understanding of Catholicism's rich intellectual and spiritual traditions. Many of their institutions struggle financially and some Catholics, including bishops, worry that these institutions are no longer clearly Catholic.

The history of the Institute for Advanced Catholic Studies tells the story of one response to the current challenges facing Catholic higher education: the formation of faculty in Catholicism as an intellectual tradition that enriches, deepens, and integrates the wide variety of academic disciplines.

*Preface*

The leaders of this initiative decided to locate this independent research institute with its own lay board of trustees on the campus of a major secular research university. Early on, some Catholic news outlets published articles condemning the Institute. Some cardinals opposed it, and one asked the Vatican to close it down.

Finding donors willing to support the development of intellectual capital rooted in Catholicism is not as easy as finding donors to support athletics, technological innovation, scholarships for poor students, entrepreneurial programs, and buildings with their names on them. Competition between Catholic universities prevented most of them from financially supporting an independent research center, even one dedicated to the intellectual and spiritual development of their own faculty.

The compelling and appealing nature of this vision has been ever more apparent, despite cultural, ecclesial, and intellectual challenges. The help of many dedicated and thoughtful people has made it possible to establish and build an independent Institute for Advanced Catholic Studies. This book tells that story and does so with gratitude.

James L. Heft, SM
June 2024

# Acknowledgments

IN THE SUBTITLE TO this history of the Institute, I describe it as a "personal" history. It could be interpreted as more autobiography than history. It is both. The truth of the matter is that by myself I would have gotten nothing done. There are many people I need to thank, starting with my religious order, the Marianists, who allowed me to leave the University of Dayton where, for the previous twenty-nine years, I had been privileged to serve in so many different capacities. I also thank the Marianists for releasing me to work on this unusual project that serves all of Catholic higher education. Thanks, too, to that first Commission on Catholic Scholars that met several times in 1998 and 1999, who hammered out the original case for and mission of the Institute, especially Michael Lacey. Members of that same Commission made it clear why we needed to locate the Institute at a nonreligiously affiliated university that wanted us and would respect the independence a research institute needs to do credible work.

I cannot begin to thank adequately the generous and dedicated board of trustees that guided the building of the Institute through difficult times (see appendix C). They also stepped up at critical moments when things were especially difficult financially and politically. I could write an essay on each and every member of the board describing how he or she contributed to realizing the Institute's mission, and on so many occasions supported me personally when things became challenging.

*Acknowledgments*

I am grateful to members of the Vatican, more specifically to then Cardinals Joseph Ratzinger and Georges Cottier who defended the Institute when two other cardinals tried to suppress it or force us to move it elsewhere. I am also thankful to Shelia Garrison, a University of Southern California graduate and recently a grandmother, for the long and faithful service she provided as my assistant. I thank the various University of Southern California development officers who helped us in raising funds for both programs and the endowment.

I am also very grateful for the comments on drafts of this history by Jan Stets, William Portier, Bro. Bernard Ploeger, Richard Wood, and Mark Roche. They all demonstrated the best of our academic community: intellectual charity and editorial candor.

One of the joys in writing this history has been the collaboration and support from Mary Brown, who was my assistant when I served as provost at the University of Dayton from 1989 to 1996. Just as she helped me make fewer mistakes as provost than I would have if left alone, she has now been a superb research assistant for me in the writing of this book. After I stepped down as provost, Mary received her master's and doctoral degrees in theological studies at the University of Dayton. In 2022, Catholic University of America Press published her superb dissertation, "Heresy in the Heartland: The Controversy at the University of Dayton, 1960–1967." It offers a granular history of a controversy between Thomists and followers of modern philosophers and theologians; basically, the controversy was between scholars with a classical vs. those with a historical approach to understanding and interpreting Church teaching. The controversy took place in the volatile period during and after Vatican II, a time marked by several controversies at various Catholic universities in the United States. I am also deeply indebted to Ryan O'Grady at the University of Dayton who prepared the grayscale and color photos for the book and the website and to another long-time friend at the University of Dayton, Kathy Martin, who volunteered and helped edit this history. Kathy served on the staff that produced alumni and internal communications for the university. Thanks, Kathy, for catching so many of my slipups! In addition to the copyediting, Kathy made other recommendations that improved the story of the Institute.

# Introduction
## A Seed Planted

SOMETIME IN THE MID-1980S, when I was chair of the University of Dayton's Religious Studies Department, a colleague of mine, Dr. William Anderson, a Presbyterian minister and a patristics scholar—one who studies the great Christian writers of the first seven centuries—told me that he thought that the Catholic Church should establish an institute for advanced studies.

Dr. William Anderson and Fr. James L. Heft in 1996

*Introduction*

Anderson also said that Catholics had a much longer intellectual tradition than Presbyterians. Over the next few years, I often returned to his suggestion. Little did I realize then that the seed he had planted would consume the next twenty-five years of my life.

In 1990, the seed sprouted and became visible. I was then the provost of the University of Dayton and was invited to give an address in San Francisco at the annual meeting of the Association of Graduate Deans of Catholic Universities. In that address, I described how Catholic higher education institutions in the United States were stand-alone entities—that is, not a coordinated and collaborative network of institutions. Instead, Catholic colleges and universities operate pretty much like the American free-enterprise system. They compete with each other for students and faculty and jealously guard their donors. Collaborating with competitors, even for a cause that would benefit both, is a form of educational bipartisanship that rarely happens. I also stated that too many Catholic colleges and universities do not have the necessary distinctive vision, scholarship, nor the educational leadership needed to support their unique intellectual mission as Catholic universities.

Recalling what Dr. Anderson said to me, I then suggested to those attending my address that what might help most would be an endowed center for advanced studies located not at a Catholic university so that it could serve all of Catholic higher education. Such a center, I went on, would make it possible for key faculty and administrators to read and think together for an extended time with leading Catholic scholars of the Catholic tradition from both Catholic and non-Catholic universities.

I do not remember how my paper was received. However, I do remember one seasoned graduate dean who said that he thought that I was dreaming to think that money could be raised for such a purpose. He reminded me that donors want to strengthen athletic teams and fund buildings with their names prominently placed on them. I knew that he was right about what motivates many people's philanthropy. What I didn't realize then was how hard it would be to raise money for intellectual work.

*Introduction*

    Not long after that, I had a conversation with Fr. Theodore Hesburgh, the legendary president of Notre Dame. When I described my idea to him, his face lit up. But then he said, "I have always wanted to do that, but I have found it very difficult to raise money to support faculty scholarship." If Ted Hesburgh wasn't able to raise money for a faculty research institute, what did I think I was going to be able to do? I wondered if that seasoned graduate dean was right—that, in fact, I had been dreaming all along.

    I never published that San Francisco address. That is why I was very surprised when in 1995 a representative of a major foundation got in touch with me to talk about Catholic higher education. What happened in the next twenty-five years turned out to be a demanding and fascinating experience, sometimes heartbreaking, but always an unusual opportunity to build an institution with a great and very much-needed mission.

# 1

# Research Institutes
# —Secular and Catholic

FROM THE TIME I began thinking about this idea, I began to learn whatever I could about institutes for advanced studies. Because my University of Dayton colleague Dr. Anderson had done his graduate studies at Princeton, he knew something about the great impact its Institute for Advanced Study has had on the scholarly community globally. In this chapter I will describe the foundation and vision of the first such institute at Princeton University, and then describe two Catholic efforts to strengthen the intellectual life among American Catholics.

Abraham Flexner (1866–1959), was the first director of the Princeton Institute for Advanced Study. He received a BA in classics at Johns Hopkins and a master's in psychology at Harvard. He spent the following year in Europe, mainly at the universities of Berlin and Heidelberg. He had a lifelong interest in educational reform. He reshaped medical education, linking the education of doctors to major universities which then established medical schools. He was most famous, however, for his leadership in establishing the Institute for Advanced Study associated with Princeton.

In 1930, Louis Bamberger and his sister Mrs. Felix Fuld gave a founding gift of $5 million to establish a research center at

Princeton University. It was founded in 1933 initially for research in physics and mathematics. By 1939, it had established three schools: mathematics, humanistic studies, and economics and politics. In 1933, Flexner was appointed the director of the Institute, a position he held until 1939. In an article published in 1939 in *Harpers* "The Usefulness of Useless Knowledge," he described the mission of the Institute as follows:

> Each school manages its own affairs as it pleases; within each group each individual disposes of his time and energy as he pleases. The members who already have come from twenty-two foreign countries and thirty-nine institutions of higher learning in the United States are admitted, if deemed worthy, by the several groups. They enjoy precisely the same freedom as the professors. They may work with this or that professor, as they severally arrange; they may work alone, consulting from time to time anyone likely to be helpful. No routine is followed; no lines are drawn between professors, members, or visitors. . . . Learning as such is cultivated. The results to the individual and to society are left to take care of themselves. No faculty meetings are held; no committees exist. Thus, men with ideas enjoy conditions favorable to reflection and to conference. . . . Men without ideas, without power of concentration on ideas, would not be at home in the Institute.[1]

Flexner understood that what scholars most treasure is time and an environment that stimulates creative thinking. He concluded his essay with a description of the Institute as a "paradise for scholars."

> We make ourselves no promises, but we cherish the hope that the unobstructed pursuit of useless knowledge will prove to have consequences in the future as in the past. Not for a moment, however, do we defend the Institute on that ground. It exists as a paradise for scholars who,

---

1. Flexner, "Usefulness," 551.

## Research Institutes—Secular and Catholic

like poets and musicians, have won the right to do as they please and who accomplish most when enabled to do so.[2]

Flexner wrote that the "justification of spiritual freedom" requires tolerance. His comment was particularly important for me as a religious person interested in fostering research that takes religion seriously, and Catholicism in particular. Having gone through the horrors of World War I and about to enter World War II, Flexner identified intolerance with race and religions. He asked,

> What could be more silly or ridiculous than likes or dislikes founded upon race or religion? Does humanity want symphonies and paintings and profound scientific truth, or does it want Christian symphonies, Christian paintings, Christian science, or Jewish symphonies, Jewish science, or Mohammedan or Egyptian or Japanese or Chinese or American or German or Russian or Communist or Conservative contributions and expressions of the infinite richness of the human soul?[3]

In the 1940s and 50s, I grew up in a family in which my mother was a Catholic and my father a Protestant who worked for a Jew, and did so happily, for over twenty-five years. The Catholic Church had not yet given official support to religious freedom, which finally it did at the Second Vatican Council (1962–1965). During the exciting years of Vatican II, I was a young Marianist religious studying philosophy, history, and theology at the University of Dayton. I knew nothing then of Abraham Flexner's assumption that religion was the enemy of tolerance, but I knew, even before Vatican II, from my mother and father's marriage that religious freedom was important. I am sure that Max Friedman, the Jew whom my father worked for, had never doubted the importance of religious freedom.

---

2. Flexner, "Usefulness," 552.
3. Flexner, "Usefulness," 550.

## CATHOLIC EFFORTS TO STRENGTHEN INTELLECTUAL LIFE

Many Catholics who immigrated to the United States in the nineteenth century had very little education. With the help of many religious orders, especially sisters' communities, Catholic elementary schools welcomed thousands of immigrants to be educated and their faith preserved in a dominantly, and sometimes hostile, Protestant country. Catholic colleges and universities, beginning with Georgetown University founded in 1789, started out as high schools. Catholic education rapidly matured. Already in 1899, Catholic educational leaders founded the Association of Catholic Colleges and Universities, followed in 1904 by the National Catholic Educational Association. Journals established by Catholic academics working in specific academic disciplines began appearing at the beginning of the twentieth century. For example, the American Catholic Historical Association was founded in 1919 and the American Catholic Sociological Association in 1938.[4] None of these Catholic professional journals featured serious interdisciplinary research, nor were any international in their membership. Existing professional associations founded by mostly Protestant faculty from major private institutions were anti-Catholic and, therefore, did not welcome Catholic scholars. Until after World War II, leading private universities, though no longer religious by then, maintained quota systems that reduced to a minimum the number of Catholics and Jews whom they would admit as students.[5] As a consequence of such anti-Catholicism, Catholic scholars talked mostly with each other. Limited in resources and marginalized by anti-Catholicism, Catholic scholars pretty much kept to themselves, often feeling the need to defend the faith against materialism and secularism.

Nevertheless, several Catholic universities established small research centers on their campuses, usually led by individuals. They

---

4. For a full listing of these Catholic organizations see Hayes, *Catholic Brain Trust*, 302, n7.

5. For further background, see Hollinger, *Science, Jews, and Secular Culture*.

rarely lasted for any length of time or produced significant scholarship. For example, in 1935, the archbishop of Cincinnati, John T. McNicholas, OP, helped to found the *Institutum Divi Thomae* (IDT) for the explicit purpose of demonstrating that science and Catholicism are not opposed.[6] A Catholic scientist, George Speri Sperti, directed the Institute. He devoted himself to research and to the education of science teachers who were also students of philosophy, a combination, it was believed, that would help prevent science education from opposing religion.

An underlying reason for establishing the IDT was to confront the perception, common in secular universities, that Catholic colleges and universities made little to no contributions to modern science and that they even opposed science. Sperti devoted his scientific efforts to creating things that immediately addressed human needs. He began by doing cancer research. But soon, his great energy embraced many different projects, some of them simply to raise money for the Institute. It had no endowment. The IDT ceased to exist in the 1950s.

## THE COMMISSION ON CATHOLIC INTELLECTUAL AND CULTURAL AFFAIRS

After World War II, a second but more significant initiative was taken to form an organization for Catholic scholars, the Catholic Commission on Intellectual and Cultural Affairs (CCICA). Unlike the IDT, it fostered serious interdisciplinary research, and became an international association of Catholic scholars devoting itself to strengthening the Catholic intellectual life in America and beyond.

If World War I was not traumatic enough to shake the confidence in the progress of Western civilization, World War II and the Cold War sent many into self-examination. Bomb shelters in backyards symbolized the "age of anxiety." For the Catholic community, the extermination of six million Jews required, on the part of Christians, deep soul searching that began to bear fruit in

---

6. Heitmann, "Doing 'True Science.'"

the Catholic Church through the Second Vatican Council (1962–1965) which condemned anti-Semitism. For American veterans of the war, the GI Bill unexpectedly and generously opened the doors to a college education—an opportunity that most Catholics, often the children of poor immigrants, never imagined was possible for them. Catholics gained greater acceptance in the still dominantly Protestant culture, though major breakthroughs would only happen with the election of John F. Kennedy in 1960 and Vatican II's affirmation of religious freedom and the separation of church and state.

In the decade preceding these breakthroughs for Catholics, leading Catholic academics lamented their lack of intellectual achievements. Catholic historian Monsignor John Tracy Ellis's explosive CCICA lecture, "American Catholics and the Intellectual Life," delivered in 1955 at its annual meeting in St. Louis was later published in the Jesuit journal *Thought*.[7] In an address given at the University of Dayton in 1994, Notre Dame historian Philip Gleason, an alumnus of the University of Dayton, described the impact of Ellis's lecture as popping "the cork on the pent-up internal forces and multiplying the shattering effect of the resulting explosion."[8]

What was it that Ellis had said that stirred things up so much? At the beginning of his essay, Ellis referred to several reputable secular scholars who deplored the state of the intellectual life in the United States. The record of Catholics was even worse, wrote Ellis. Part of the problem was that the staggering number of immigrants were reduced to learning a new language, getting jobs, and feeding their families. But he also held Catholic leadership responsible. He cited, for example, Archbishop Cushing's 1947 statement taking pride that all the bishops he knew were from working class families. He was also critical of Catholic higher education where very few scholars had won fellowships, and few Catholic universities even thought about building endowments. He lamented that faculty at Princeton, Chicago, and the University of Virginia

---

7. Ellis, "American Catholics," 351–388.
8. Gleason, "Catholic Identity," 16–17.

contributed to the renewal of scholastic philosophy while faculty at Catholic universities did little.

Ellis cited the particularly incriminating remarks of the president of the University of Chicago, Robert M. Hutchins, who, in 1937 in an address to a group of Catholic educators at Catholic universities, told them they had failed to make the Catholic intellectual tradition the center of their curricula, even though Catholicism had the longest "intellectual tradition of any institution in the contemporary world." Hutchins criticized Catholic higher education because it had "imitated the worst features of secular education and ignored most of the good ones."[9] Instead, it mistakenly invested in athletics, vocationalism and anti-intellectualism. Except for a few women's colleges, the offerings and the scholarship in the humanities were weak. Finally, Ellis described the pointless competition, even bordering on "internecine warfare," which prevented Catholic universities from pooling resources to found good graduate programs. Ellis concluded his essay by placing blame not on anti-Catholicism but on Catholics themselves for their "failure to have measured up to their responsibilities to the comparable tradition of Catholic learning of which they are the direct heirs."[10]

Ellis was neither the first nor the only critic of the academic mediocrity of Catholic higher education. Already in the 1920s and 1930s, Catholics like George Shuster and Fr. John A. O'Brien lamented the Catholic community's absence of scholarship, especially in science. Ellis's 1955 essay, however, evoked a deeper and more widespread process of soul searching for the entire Catholic higher education community.

Also during the 1920s and 1930s, Pope Pius XI (1922–1939) called upon the laity to support the hierarchy in its efforts to spread the gospel. Called the Catholic Action movement, the pope invited the laity to join with the hierarchy in their efforts to stem the tide of secularism and materialism that became ever more prevalent in the twentieth century, especially in Europe. It called

---

9. Ellis, "American Catholics," 375.
10. Ellis, "American Catholics," 386.

for "the participation of the laity in the apostolate of the Church's hierarchy."[11] It would take a few more decades for the Church to make it clear that not only the hierarchy, but also the laity had an apostolate, one that was distinct from that of the hierarchy. How best to understand the appropriate autonomy and responsibility of the laity underwent major changes at Vatican II where it was declared that not only priests and religious were called to holiness, but everyone, by their baptism, is also called and has a mission to evangelize. Few lay people then, and for that matter still today, felt that they were educated enough to evangelize.

Once the GI Bill opened the doors for World War II veterans, Catholic colleges and universities began to develop courses in theology for lay students. Until that time, professors taught religion and especially the philosophy of Saint Thomas Aquinas (1225–1274) to keep Catholic college students faithful to the Church. Before the 1950s, theology courses were taught only to seminarians while the laity were taught religion, mostly in the form of apologetics—how best to defend the faith of Catholics in a Protestant country.

The shift in the 1950s to teaching undergraduates theology required that faculty prepare themselves to teach theology, which in turn called for extensive faculty development. They had to learn how to teach theology, not as it was taught to seminarians, but as it needed to be taught to lay students.[12] Even though the quality of scholarship at most Catholic colleges and universities was still limited, faculty at these institutions began to think through how to educate the laity in new ways.

After World War II, the CCICA was founded to address the lack of intellectual achievement among American Catholic scholars. Patrick Hayes, a historian and archivist, has done a great service in writing a magisterial history of this most significant post–World War II effort by Catholic scholars to create a stronger intellectual life in and for the Church: *A Catholic Brain Trust: The*

---

11. Pius XI, "Discourse," 14.
12. Mize, *Joining*.

*History of the Catholic Commission on Intellectual and Cultural Affairs, 1945–1965*. What follows will be drawn mainly from Hayes's study.

According to the 1917 Code of Canon Law, any organization that included the word *Catholic* required the approval of a bishop.[13] Acquiring such approval was easier when religious and priests were leading the formation of such institutions. Priests and religious were accountable to bishops and their religious superiors. How to understand the accountability of laity in leadership roles in the Church was less clear and still remains a point of contention and confusion.

Founded in 1946, the leaders of the CCICA debated not only about the proper relationship they should have with the bishops, but also about how closely the CCICA should work with existing Catholic organizations such as the National Catholic Educational Association and the National Catholic Welfare Council, as well as with international organizations such as Pax Romana and Unitas.[14] A leading intellectual at the time, Jesuit John Courtney Murray, argued that since the membership of the CCICA would mainly be lay scholars, they would have to think carefully about acquiring

---

13. Peters, "Title 18," Canon 688.

14. The National Catholic Educational Association was founded in 1904 as a unifying agent for Catholic education at the national level. Today, it is the largest private professional education association in the world. The National Catholic Welfare Council was the annual meeting of the US bishops and its secretariat. In 1919, it succeeded the National Catholic War Council, an emergency organization. Around 1922, the name was changed from Council to Conference. The latter split into the National Conference of Catholic Bishops and the United States Catholic Conference. In 2001, both groups reunited as the United States Conference of Catholic Bishops. *Pax Romana* consists of two organizations: the International Movement of Catholic Students founded in 1921 in Switzerland and the International Catholic Movement for Intellectual and Cultural Affairs. Both encourage their members to think, reflect, and act on issues facing the world and the Church. *Pax Romana* has consultative status with UNESCO and has permanent delegates at the United Nations in New York and Geneva and with UNESCO. *Unitas*: the Catholic League for the Unity of Christians is an organization founded by the Church of England and dedicated to the full visible reconciliation of Anglicans and Roman Catholics as one Church. The League is ecumenical in membership.

the approval of the bishops in such a way that their organization could protect the necessary independence and academic freedom to do their scholarly work. Collaboration with non-Catholic organizations, such as the United Nations Educational, Scientific and Cultural Organization (UNESCO) would, and quickly did, prove tricky when, in 1946, Julian Huxley, the director general, published a pamphlet that supported eugenics, evolution, and various forms of materialism.[15]

Besides the challenge of cooperating in an appropriate way with non-Catholic organizations, the leaders of the CCICA knew they needed a degree of independence within the Church. Murray wrote that they would be "crippled at the outset if the hierarchy is moving in."[16] In late 1945, he argued strongly for the CCICA to be an "autonomous body, which will have influence by reason of its own intrinsic excellence." He hoped that they could "get at least a negative approval ('we do not disapprove') from the bishops" for collaboration with non-Catholic groups.[17]

Besides the importance of greater freedom for scholarly work, the CCICA also worried that the leadership of lay scholars would make some bishops nervous. In a discussion about the formation of an editorial board for the updated *Catholic Encyclopedia for the American Church*, Cardinal Stritch wanted the majority to be priests. One might think that after Vatican II this tension between the bishops and lay-led Catholic research organizations would largely disappear. As we shall see, this hardly proved to be the case, even at the beginning of the twenty-first century.

Besides the challenge of establishing an appropriate relationship with non-Catholic organizations and with the bishops, the CCICA also faced the challenge of how to organize itself. The first task was to name an executive director, and then determine what

---

15. Hayes, *Catholic Brain Trust*, 83. The constitution of UNESCO was adopted in 1945 for the purpose of bringing people together and strengthening the "intellectual and moral solidarity of humankind through mutual understanding and dialogue between cultures." History of UNESCO, para. 2. https://www.unesco.org/en/history.

16. Hayes, *Catholic Brain Trust*, 31.

17. Hayes, *Catholic Brain Trust*, 20.

could be expected of him. They assumed that the leader needed to be a cleric. They also discussed what support he would need and where his office should be located.

The first executive director was Fr. Edward Stanford, OSA (1945–1953), who had served as president of Villanova University from 1932–1944 and then as prior and rector of Augustinian College in Washington, DC, 1944–1950. From 1950 to 1959, he served as the principal and superior of the Augustinian Community at Archbishop Carroll High School, also located in Washington, DC. He never received any salary as the executive director of the CCICA and, at one point, expressed during his last four years some displeasure about this.

The next executive director, Fr. William J. Rooney (1954–1983), taught English at the Catholic University of America. For the next twenty-eight years, the only office he had was the one he had as an English professor. He remained an assistant professor all those years, burdened with a full teaching schedule and directing several doctoral students. He had no money to hire a secretary. Like Fr. Stanford, for many years he did not receive any salary for his services.

Three things should become obvious from this description of the responsibilities and working conditions of the first two executive directors. First, that money was tight: both men already had full-time jobs, neither had assistants for CCICA work, and, except for a small stipend of $1,500 that Rooney began to receive more than halfway through his work, neither was ever paid a salary. No consideration was given to hiring a lay scholar since they knew that they could never pay him a suitable salary. Moreover, as we have already seen, before Vatican II a layman directing an entity like the CCICA would make some bishops raise questions about their authority and the layman's accountability.

During the first few years, the membership dues were only five dollars. The decision to increase dues was postponed until the organization could get better organized and create a financial plan that would support its ambitions.[18] The members of the CCICA

---

18. Hayes, *Catholic Brain Trust*, 65.

never realized the dream of a financially and ecclesiastically independent research center led by laypersons. In short, financial realities drastically limited what the CCICA accomplished.

Second, both executive directors worked within Catholic institutions. It had to be embarrassing to the founders of the CCICA when, in 1963, Catholic University of America graduate students invited four periti of Vatican II to speak on campus: John Courtney Murray and Gustave Weigel,[19] both Jesuits and members of the CCICA, Benedictine Father Godfrey Diekmann, and the Swiss theologian and diocesan priest Hans Küng. The university cancelled the lecture series with the explanation that the topics they were to speak about were still not the final teachings of the Second Vatican Council. This unfortunate incident and the excuse for the cancellation reminded members of the CCICA that, for many bishops, all scholarship had to be "safe."

Third, one has to admire and applaud the generosity of Stanford and Rooney who found ways to devote as much of their time as they could to the CCICA mission and organize their various conferences and on-going research. Despite their many responsibilities, they and the members of the CCICA helped bring to the United States Catholic scholars from Europe. They also supported John Courtney Murray's scholarship on the church/state issue and religious freedom that bore fruit at Vatican II, despite the ultimately unsuccessful efforts of two faculty members at the Catholic University of America who, during the 1950s, criticized Murray's work, reporting him and his work to the Vatican. The CCICA gave some excellent guidance to the *New Catholic Encyclopedia* project that finally saw its publication only after Vatican II. They also committed themselves to the development of younger Catholic scholars. They sponsored John Tracy Ellis's explosive 1955 speech. They explored alliances with non-Catholic institutions such as UNESCO, but found it difficult to support some of its assumptions, including a form of evolution that excluded divine participation.

19. Weigel, "Gustave Weigel." Fr. Weigel wrote his own entry in *The Book of Catholic Authors*.

Even if the dream of the founders of the CCICA did not come to fruition, several statements of some of its members continued to inspire later efforts to build the Institute for Advanced Catholic Studies. For example, in 1956, Jacques Maritain stated that a small group of gifted scholars could make a major contribution to strengthening Catholic scholarship and its intellectual tradition. He thought that it was only through such groups that

> any genuine work of intellectual integration and of restoration of value can be undertaken and bear fruit. I am dreaming of small institutes in which a certain number of young people really capable of creative work, and selected as intelligently as possible, would be given all facilities to pursue disinterested research in any field whatsoever, on the sole condition that they would at the same time acquire, under the guidance of some competent masters, deep personal knowledge of Christian philosophy and theology, and that they would also pursue a steady conversation among themselves about their various activities, so as to achieve some kind of common understanding, common language and intellectual cooperation.[20]

If one removes Maritain's reference to the importance of Christian philosophy and theology, his description actually echoes Abraham Flexner's 1939 description of how scholars should work together, the free time they should enjoy, and the disinterested type of research that could lead to groundbreaking discoveries. Perhaps Maritain, having been at Princeton, was influenced by its Institute for Advanced Study. He even may have read Flexner's famous 1939 essay. Hayes, in his otherwise extensive history of CCICA, does not say anything about whether Flexner's ideas and Princeton's Institute for Advanced Study may have influenced Maritain's dream.

Vatican II brought about so many changes in the understanding of the role of the laity, ecumenical and interreligious dialogue, religious freedom, and a new emphasis on the *sensus fidelium* (sense of the faithful) that the founding purposes of the CCICA began to

---

20. Hayes, *Catholic Brain Trust*, 228.

seem less needed. By the late sixties, major Catholic universities promoted faculty governance, granted tenure, and established lay boards of trustees. No one predicted that the religious orders that had founded and built 90 percent of the US Catholic colleges and universities, would then suffer dramatic losses of personnel. By the early 1980s, Saint Pope John Paul II started a process to clarify the mission of Catholic universities that resulted in his 1990 apostolic constitution on Catholic universities, *Ex Corde Ecclesiae*. But that is a whole new and different story.

After celebrating its fiftieth anniversary in 1995, the CCICA officially closed down when its final executive director, Daniel Burke, published a pamphlet titled *The Catholic Commission: A Sketch of Its Early Years*. It is telling that he concluded his pamphlet without any suggestions for how it might or should continue. Hayes mentioned that the executive committee confided the future of the organization to Scott Appleby, a historian at the University of Notre Dame.[21] It was around 1995 that Appleby and David O'Brien, a historian at Holy Cross College, came to the University of Dayton and asked me if I would assume the leadership of the CCICA. It was an honor to be asked. I already knew something of its history, but having served by that time a number of years as provost of the University of Dayton, I was very aware of the amount of money that would be needed to support first-rate scholarship and build a residential center for extended sabbaticals. I remember telling them that I would consider their offer if they could raise a $2 million endowment which, I explained, would support an executive director part-time and an assistant full-time in such an effort. They admitted they could not do that, required as they were to raise money only for their own universities. The CCICA ceased to exist.

---

21. Hayes, *Catholic Brain Trust*, 282–83.

# 2

# Collaborating to Build a New Institution

AT THE TIME APPLEBY and O'Brien visited me, I was already thinking about another way to strengthen Catholic intellectual life. I knew that a new initiative needed to be different from the IDT and CCICA. Standing at the beginning of the twenty-first century, the increasing number of lay scholars, coupled with the loss of so many of the religious mentioned previously, the intellectual life of the Church and Catholic higher education remained a major concern of mine, especially as it related to the formation of Catholic intellectuals. Measured by secular standards, the academic quality of many of the Catholic colleges and universities had increased, but the strength of the Catholic intellectual tradition in their faculty and the distinctiveness of their curriculum had not. I believed and still believe that the greatest need is an independent research center that would help scholars embrace Catholicism as an intellectual tradition relevant in different ways to all the academic disciplines.

During the first stages of planning for the Institute for Advanced Catholic Studies, I kept in mind the observation of Notre Dame historian Philip Gleason, echoing John Tracy Ellis's 1955 critique of Catholic higher education, that Catholic colleges and universities in the United States suffered from localism, a provincialism that made genuine collaboration between them difficult. Expecting Catholic universities to pool funds to support an independent research institute dedicated to the service of all of their scholars would gain no traction. There is, however, the exception of the president of one university which I will describe later.

By the 1970s, the intellectual impact and quality of the publications of faculty who were fellows at various institutes for advanced studies shaped much of the intellectual life of the country and beyond. While many smaller research centers have been established on various US campuses, the most influential research institutes are secular and independent organizations. I have already described the Princeton Institute for Advanced Study founded in 1933. Another institute, the Center for Advanced Study in the Behavioral Sciences was founded in 1954 in Palo Alto. Still another influential center devoted to the study of government and international relations, the Woodrow Wilson Center, was founded in Washington, DC in 1968. Finally, the National Humanities Center was founded in Research Triangle Park, North Carolina in 1978. All are funded privately except for the one in DC, which the government funds. None of these research centers focuses on the study of religion.

I mentioned earlier that I did not publish the paper that I presented in 1990 in San Francisco to graduate deans of Catholic universities. Someone who attended that talk must have told the leadership of the Argidius Foundation, a Catholic foundation in Europe, about my idea. At that time, this foundation was interested in supporting initiatives that would strengthen both the quality of scholarship and develop a clearer understanding of religious identity of Catholic colleges and universities. One of the leaders of that foundation contacted me in the spring of 1995, the same year I was offered the leadership of the CCICA, and invited me to discuss how they, as a foundation, might address the most pressing needs of Catholic higher education in the United States. They were especially interested in preventing the secularization of Catholic higher education by strengthening Catholic identity and the quality of Catholic scholarship.

The foundation was already considering several proposals. They showed these proposals to me and asked for my evaluation of them. After a few months of conversation with them, they asked me to be their principal advisor. In the fall of 1995, leaders of the foundation visited the University of Dayton. I told them that I was planning to step down as provost the following year and would assume a new position, the university professor of faith and culture and chancellor. The new position would allow me to work on faculty development and represent the university at the national level. I told them that I would then have more time to evaluate the various projects the foundation was considering. To ensure that I would have the time needed to do what they were asking, they met with then-President Bro. Raymond Fitz, SM, who supported the foundation's plan to fund 25 percent of my time, as well as support a full-time executive assistant.

My modest record of scholarship was not at the level needed to make me a scholar who could be admitted to one of the existing national research centers. In working on the vision for IACS, I needed someone who had stronger academic credentials than I—someone who also cared about strengthening Catholic intellectual life. I thought of Dr. Michael Lacey. I immediately got in touch with him. He not only was an excellent scholar and cared about increasing the quality of Catholic scholarship but was also the director of the Division of US Studies at the Woodrow Wilson International Center for Scholars.

Lacey first came to my attention in 1991 when, at the annual convention of the Catholic Theological Society of America, he gave a major address, "The Backwardness of American Catholicism." He identified two major causes of the backwardness of Catholic scholars in America: an *ambivalence* toward high-level research by Catholic universities themselves and an *ambiguity* of the Church's (the hierarchy and most of the laity) commitment to the growth of knowledge. He saw no point for Catholic colleges and universities to be like Harvard or Yale, losing their distinctive missions and following down the road to secularization already trod by most major Protestant universities.

Rather, he recommended the establishment of "some kind of institute for advanced study to be devoted to the needs of Catholic scholars in all of the humanities and the social sciences, and to involve the participation in governance of both clerical and lay people." He also recommended that such an institute not be located at a Catholic university so that it "might address the needs of the system as a whole and not succumb to the underlying problems of localism, decentralism, and the embarrassing inability to cooperate that have beset the Catholic system from the beginning."[1] I told him about the foundation that was interested in backing in a major way the creation of an independent Catholic research institute, and asked for his help. He graciously agreed. We worked closely together for the next eight years (1995 through late 2003).

The foundation welcomed Lacey as my key collaborator and advisor in this project. We both spent time with the leaders of the foundation explaining why we thought the establishment of an independent Catholic institute for advanced studies would be the most promising option. In a letter dated September 5, 1996, they asked us to develop a concept paper, a prospectus, that would be "very clear about the national need for such an independent center, and how, through its purpose(s) and activities (e.g., research, fellowships, conferences, summer institutes, mentoring programs, publications) this need would be addressed. The expected impact of these activities on the intended beneficiaries, direct and indirect, should also be explained." The foundation listed several points they wanted the prospectus to address:

- How the center would help make the Catholic faith respectable in academic circles, which are so used to secular discourse only.
- How it would help alleviate fears of dogmatism, authoritarianism, and proselytism among non-Catholic scholars regarding the Catholic intellectual tradition.

1. Lacey, "Backwardness," 13–15.

- How it would demonstrate that essential to the Catholic faith is respect for other religious traditions which search for the truth and recognize the existence of a transcendent force beyond human comprehension.
- How it would serve to induce young talented scholars to pursue an academic career in Catholic higher education.
- How it would encourage mentorship between recognized Catholic scholars in specific academic fields and talented up-and-coming young Christian scholars.

The reason why the foundation requested that we make a clear case for a national independent institution was that other leaders in Catholic higher education had offered different ideas to address the needs of Catholic colleges and universities. For example, two presidents of major Jesuit universities believed that the research institute should be located on the campus of a major Catholic university; unsurprisingly, both suggested that their own universities would be the best location for it.

Over the Christmas holidays of 1996, Lacey and I worked together on the prospectus, with Lacey doing most of the heavy lifting. The text went through several drafts. An edited version of it was ready by February 1997 (see appendix A). At the time, I was also serving as the board chair of the Association of Catholic Colleges and Universities. Lacey and I asked the board, comprised mainly of presidents of US Catholic colleges and universities, to endorse our proposal. After a spirited conversation, they voted unanimously to support it. Once the foundation had read the prospectus and met again with Lacey and me, they agreed that, indeed, the best option for rejuvenating Catholic scholarship was the establishment of an independent, international institution that would serve all of Catholic higher education and be located at a non-Catholic university.

Getting high profile endorsements for the project were as important as they were difficult to obtain, especially from leaders of Catholic universities who feared that we might compete with them or steal their donors. For example, on February 1, 1999,

Lacey and I were invited to a board meeting of the Association of Jesuit Colleges and Universities to speak about the Institute. We hoped that they would endorse the project. When the president of the board made a motion to that effect, no one seconded it. One week later, we received a nice letter from the president encouraging us and wishing us success with our project, but it contained no endorsement.

The next step was to invite prominent Catholic scholars to vet the prospectus and begin figuring out how to organize and locate it. In February 1997, the foundation set aside $800,000 to bring together twenty-five scholars and influential Catholic leaders for the task. Almost every leader in Catholic scholarship and education whom we invited to help us accepted our invitation to come together to discuss the idea. Besides scholars such as Charles Taylor, John Noonan, Monika Hellwig, Katarina Schuth, OSF, and David Tracy, we invited several college presidents and interested business leaders, such as Paul Caron, a Georgetown graduate and the former vice president of J. P. Morgan's operations in Europe. Caron became an important member of the Institute's inaugural board of trustees. We also invited Scott Appleby and David O'Brien to help us. The response of the invitees was enthusiastic, especially when they learned the foundation was giving serious consideration to supporting this project with matching dollars to the level of $25 million. For every million we could raise, they would match it with another million. Late 1997 and all of 1998 were very busy years for thinking through the mission of the Institute with this larger group.

We named this group the Commission on Catholic Scholarship (CCS) (see appendix B). We held an initial one-day meeting in the Pittsburgh airport in early May 1997. The meeting had two purposes: first, to clarify the mission as outlined and developed in the prospectus, and second, to decide how best to proceed. We created five subcommittees: Scholarly Focus and Programs, Long-Term Finance and Budget, Location and Facilities, Institutional Coordination and Cooperation, and Governance and Staffing. We had several meetings over the following year. All the committees also held conference calls and received funding if they needed to travel. At the next two meetings, the members of the CCS thoroughly discussed the subcommittees' reports and recommendations.

The next in-person meeting of the CCS took place in Washington, DC on February 13 and 14, 1998. The Scholarly Focus and Programs Committee, which had received copies of the prospectus for discussion, called for greater clarification of the meaning of the *Catholic tradition*, asked for further discussion on some of the ideas of the prospectus, and strongly recommended that the Institute be free-standing and independent (not controlled by any Catholic university nor by the US bishops).

Questions were also raised about how best to describe its independence. Although all the members of the commission came to agree on the importance of independence for the Institute, they were also aware that its independence needed careful articulation to avoid needless controversy, especially with some members of the Catholic episcopal community. As it turned out, we had underestimated the opposition that would come from some members of the Church. Eventually, the committee offered the following explanation of the Institute's independence:

> While the Institute will be bound by its own charter and governed by its own board of directors, it intends to carry out its work in the communion of the Church and knows that its success requires the support and encouragement of the hierarchy, representatives of which will serve as advisors to the Institute.[2]

Though the committee was confident that the Institute would remain in relationship with the Catholic Church, some felt it wasn't clear enough how. Not too many months from then, some people were claiming that the Institute wanted no such relationship, and even that it was not canonically possible for a Catholic institute to be launched without the permission and approval of a bishop. I will describe these criticisms and assertions in more detail later. Suffice

2. Joseph A. Komonchak, email to the author, November 8, 1998.

it to say here that after consulting the opinions of two prominent Catholic canon lawyers early in 2001, Sister Sharon Euart, RSM, and Fr. Ladislas Örsy, SJ, we were assured that current canon law allowed for an independent, lay-led, research institute.

We asked them if it was necessary that, for the Institute for Advanced Catholic Studies to be Catholic, it be jurisdictionally related to the bishop. Euart assured us that while the use of the word *Catholic* required ecclesiastical consent ("a sort of 'truth in advertising' requirement by the Catholic Church"),[3] that did not, however, subject the Institute as an initiative of the faithful to any more jurisdiction than consent to use the name *Catholic*. Örsy's reply was similar. He explained that a local bishop could approve the Institute as a private association subject to the vigilance of that bishop. Vigilance, he added, is a rather negative power; the bishop is entitled to intervene when he has evidence that something is going wrong: "He has no right to impose any specific rule or policy but he can request information necessary to exercise his 'vigilance.'"[4] Both responses, we believed, affirmed that we did not need to be jurisdictionally related to a bishop, though a bishop, after careful examination, could deny the Institute's description of itself as Catholic. A bishop also had the power, after careful examination and with good reason, to order the Institute to leave his diocese as long as it insisted on retaining *Catholic* in its name.

One member of the commission summarized our finding by referring to documents of Vatican II, the two legal opinions we had solicited, and consulting the newly revised 1983 Code of Canon Law.[5] He distinguished three types of ecclesial organizations: a hierarchical mission in which the laity are fully subject to episcopal jurisdictional control; a hierarchical mandate that leaves the laity their appropriate freedom to act on their own initiative; and finally, "enterprises that are established by the free choice of the laity and

---

3. Sharon Euart, RSM, Canonical Opinion on the Canonical Status of the Institute for Advanced Catholic Studies, February 20, 2001, 5.

4. Ladislas Örsy, SJ, letter to author, March 2, 2001.

5. See especially John Paul II, "Title V."

are governed by their prudent judgement."[6] Such enterprises need the approval of a bishop to call themselves Catholic. The Institute, an example of the third model, required the least formal relationship with a bishop.[7]

Finally, the committee recommended that a stronger focus be placed on understanding the impact of American culture on the Catholic faith, and that criteria be developed for the selection of scholars for the Institute and the types of appointments to be made. One of the members of the committee reported that when visiting Princeton's Institute for Advanced Study, a long-time member of its staff recommended strongly that we do not make any permanent appointments; such appointments create, in his words, "too many extinct volcanoes."

The Governance Committee recommended the formation of a lay board of trustees and an Academic Advisory Council. For the membership of the board, they recommended that it would be best to have three types of persons to serve on the board: academics who could keep the mission focused intellectually, people of means who understood and could support the mission financially, and finally "amphibians"—that is, college presidents or provosts and deans who were used to working with both donors and faculty and understood how to keep the conversations between them positive and productive. By the summer of 2000, we had established our first official board of trustees with nine members, along with an international Academic Advisory Council that included a group of distinguished scholars (see appendix C). The following year we would add Jill Ker Conway and Ellen Hancock, who for many years chaired the board and became one of its major donors. Both Conway and Hancock would play a critical role in the survival of the Institute at one of its most vulnerable moments.[8]

6. Paul VI, *Apostolicam Actuositatem*, para. 24.
7. See also John Paul II, "Title I," Canon 216.
8. Jill Ker Conway is the former president of Smith College and a historian who did her doctorate at Harvard and has served on many boards, including Merrill Lynch. Ellen Hancock was a technology executive with IBM, National Semiconductor Corp., and Apple Computing before serving as CEO of Exodus Communications, Inc. and president of Jazz Technologies, Inc. She, too, served

The Finance and Budget Committee decided to interview three companies that had donor-prospect research capabilities. While the members of the committee admired the fifteen-page, double-columned prospectus, they recommended that we create a more succinct statement of our objectives and purposes accessible to the wider public. The first document we created to meet this recommendation was titled "Commonly Asked Questions About the Institute for Advanced Catholic Studies." It contained responses to sixteen questions that we thought would offer a clear understanding of the nature and mission of the Institute. It turned out to be eight pages long. Though pleased with the effort, members of the commission felt it was still too academic and not easily accessible to potential donors, most of whom would, of course, not be academics. One consultant said we needed a clear and compelling elevator speech—that is, something that could be said and understood in a very short time, like going from floor one to floor four. We finally produced a single-page, folded brochure that on one side stated, in two short paragraphs, the need for the Institute, and on the opposite side described, also in simple sentences, the benefits. We listed four beneficiaries: the Church, Catholic colleges and universities, scholars working in the Catholic tradition, and society (see appendix D).

We soon discovered that it was also difficult to find professional fundraisers who understood the need for and the mission of the Institute. Donations for scholarships for poor students, buildings, athletics and dormitories are much easier to raise. As Fr. Hesburgh had told me earlier, it is very difficult to raise money to support faculty research. A wealthy conservative potential donor once said to me, "Why should I give money to support liberal scholars who will write books criticizing how I have built my fortune?" Communicating the mission of the Institute in a compelling manner to non-academics remained a difficult challenge.

The Location Committee unanimously agreed that the Institute should not be located at a Catholic university. Rather, it

---

on numerous boards including that of Marist College. She died on April 19, 2022.

needed to be located at a major, nonreligiously affiliated research university that wanted us. Early on, I had thought about locating the Institute in Europe. We decided to arrange meetings with two leading European cardinals to seek their advice. On December 2, 1998, Scott Appleby, a member of the CCS, and I met with Cardinal Godfried Maria Jules Danneels of Belgium (elevated to cardinal in 1983) and then on March 3, 1999 with a second cardinal, Carlo Maria Martini of Milan, Italy (also elevated to cardinal in 1983). I had sent them information about the Institute several weeks before our meetings. I also sent them a copy of the newly drafted prospectus. It was obvious during these meetings that both cardinals had read carefully what I had sent them. Cardinal Martini had actually typed out a series of good questions that he gave me; unfortunately, I can no longer find it. However, I do remember one question that he, with a slight smile, asked me at the end of our interview: "What assurance do you have, Father, that this institute will not produce scholarship that could cause scandal in the Church?" I remember this moment in our conversation vividly. I replied, "With all due respect, your eminence, what assurance do you have that someone you have recruited to the priesthood, sent to your seminary, and then ordained will not cause a scandal for the Church?" Even as I was saying this, I thought that I had crossed the line of episcopal etiquette. I was relieved when the cardinal smiled and said, "Good answer."

Both cardinals agreed, however, that wherever we locate the Institute, it should not be in Europe! I remember in particular Martini saying that if we locate it in Germany, the Italians and French scholars won't go, and if we established it in Italy, very few of the top scholars from the rest of Europe would go. He added, "If you locate it in the United States, it will not only be better run but most of the scholars in Europe would want to go, even if some of them looked down on the US for its alleged lack of Catholic intellectuals." Danneels stressed repeatedly that the scholarship had to be at the highest *niveau*, the highest level. He said that there were too many mediocre Catholic institutes throughout Europe. Both also mentioned that, in the United States, donors received tax deductions for philanthropic activity which encouraged the wealthy to be generous. In Europe, Martini added, governments supply most support for most organizations, but rarely any religious ones. In short, fundraising in Europe for the Institute would be very difficult, much more difficult than in the United States.

The committee on Location agreed with the two cardinals and looked instead at possible cities for the Institute in North America. They visited ten major research universities, none of which had any religious affiliation. They recommended Berkeley, Chicago, Washington, Boston, and Princeton. The committee first visited Princeton where a group of bright and energetic Catholic scholars were very much engaged in some of the debates going on about the Church in the United States, especially abortion. We had already distinguished in our planning between a think-tank and a research institute. In terms of Catholicism, the former would be dedicated to promoting a preferred version of Catholicism, whereas a research institute would support basic research in Catholicism—research that included many different points of view. Instead of promoting a liberal or conservative view of the Church, a research institute would support excellent scholars who would be free to publish the results of the work whether flattering to or critical of the Church. Finally, we also learned that the administration of Princeton had no interest in the Institute, just a few of its faculty.

We then visited Yale University, or more specifically, the Catholic Campus Ministry of Yale University. Like Princeton, they, too, had several prominent Catholic intellectuals involved on their board and in their programming. The campus ministry at Yale thought that the Institute would offer a wonderful complement to their own programming. Yale's Catholic Campus Ministry was and remains nationally known for its vibrancy, leadership, and programming. They had just recently received a $50 million gift from a Yale alum and were in the process of building a new student center. They offered to add a third floor for the Institute. It was an attractive offer at a place with a vital religious presence for its students. But there were several drawbacks. First, there was no interest in the Institute on the part of the university. Second, the

Institute's mission was to engage faculty directly and only students indirectly through faculty. It would also be harder to keep the intellectual and research mission clear and distinct from the mission of campus ministry if the Institute was located on the top floor of a new building of a stellar Catholic campus ministry program.

Third, we wanted to avoid the tendency most donors would have that the mission of the Institute was to help college students understand and keep the faith. We believed that helping students in that way was important but wanted to work directly with scholars who would teach students for decades.

A number of Catholic colleges and universities had created Catholic Studies programs that we thought might create a fourth misunderstanding of the Institute's mission. Catholic Studies programs at their best expose students to Catholicism in more robust ways through a variety of academic disciplines rather than assuming that one or two required theology or religious studies courses would be sufficient for student education and formation in Catholicism. We were already concerned that our working title for the Institute, The Institute for Advanced Catholic Studies, could be confused with these undergraduate programs. Adding the word *advanced*, we later found out, didn't clarify the Institute's mission for most people. People identify a new and unusual institute with entities they already know. For various reasons the other possible locations were also ruled out.

It was at that moment, providentially, that John Noonan, judge of the US Court of Appeals for the Ninth Circuit, recommended we take a look at the University of Southern California (USC) in Los Angeles, a private, nonreligiously affiliated university founded in 1880 as a Methodist institution. It now enrolled fifty thousand students. Frankly, I was surprised at the recommendation, even though USC is a major, well-respected, research university. Over the years, I had been to LA several times to speak at various events and was overwhelmed with the traffic and its ubiquitous freeways, some with eight and even nine lanes going one way. Noonan had said that the university leadership was interested in us locating there. After some discussion, we agreed to visit USC.

It turned out that Noonan was a good friend with historian Kevin Starr, a fellow San Franciscan with whom he had been talking about the Institute. Starr was on the faculty of USC and had already talked with some of the university's leadership about the Institute. They were enthusiastic to have the Institute on their campus. Four members of the commission, Lacey, Noonan, Fr. John Coleman, SJ, and I visited the campus. I never expected the welcome we received and the depth of their understanding of the mission of the Institute. They had carefully prepared and had already studied the mission statement. The first evening we were there, a dinner was organized by Joseph Aoun, the dean of the College of Letters, Arts, and Sciences (and later the president of Northeastern University in Boston), and attended by Neil Pings, the provost of the university (previously on the faculty of Cal Tech), and Thomas Condon, a graduate of a Marianist high school in Los Angeles. Condon, along with four others, was the founder and manager of Providence Investment Council, a very successful investment management company, and later became a board member of the Institute and one of its major donors. All three are Catholic.

The next evening, Steven Sample, the president of the university, held a banquet for us at the president's mansion in San Marino, a suburb north of downtown Los Angeles. He had invited several USC board members, major university administrators, and leaders of Los Angeles, including Robert Erburu, the chairman of Times Mirror Co., the parent company of the *Los Angeles Times*, and a prominent Catholic in Los Angeles, and John Argue, the chair of USC's Board of Trustees. It was an extraordinary evening. At least ten of the people the president had invited each gave short speeches, including Tom Condon, who spoke last. They all explained why it made great sense for the Institute to locate at USC. It became clear why USC wanted us. First, they were ranked at that time the fifteenth top university in the United States. Their ambition, however, was to be in the top ten. To be a top research university required, among other things, the production of original research. That is exactly what the Institute would do. Second, our institute would fill a hole in their programs related to the study of religion. They had two relatively small centers for Jewish scholarship and were planning to launch a major research program in Muslim studies. The only Christian center they had at USC focused mainly on pastoral and ecumenical issues in the city of Los Angeles. President Sample, a Protestant, later said to me what my colleague at the University of Dayton, Dr. William Anderson, told me in 1985, "You Catholics have the long intellectual tradition. That's why I prefer a Catholic research center."

President Sample played such an important role in the history of the Institute that something more should be said about him. At the age of twenty-four, he earned a doctorate in engineering and became a faculty member at Purdue. But he was restless. He loved the arts and literature, history, and philosophy. As an engineer, he created and patented the digital controls that became the buttons people punch when operating microwave ovens. At twenty-nine, he was encouraged by a colleague to apply for the executive assistant position to Purdue's president. He loved it. He acquired promotions at the University of Illinois and the University of Nebraska and, in 1982, at the age of forty-one, became the president of the University of Buffalo, part of the State University of New York (SUNY) system. He heard a board member call the University of Buffalo the "university of last resort" and had trouble finding students who were proud of their university. Sample was determined to turn things around, and did so by transforming the University of Buffalo into a major national research university recognized by the school's election into the Association of American Universities, a prestigious group of top research universities.

In 1991 Sample became president of USC, a private university and one that also needed a major turnaround. It was referred to as the "university of second choice." Using a unique leadership style, later laid out in *The Contrarian's Guide to Leadership* published in 2001, his theories were tested when, in the first year of his presidency, shortfalls in tuition required him to lay off 8 percent of the staff just a few months after he had arrived. The televised police beating of Rodney King on March 3, 1991, and the subsequent riots that broke out in South Los Angeles posed another challenge. USC is located on a huge city block that begins at West Thirty-Fourth Street. Alums and trustees exerted great pressure to relocate the university as Pepperdine had done when, after the 1965 Watts riots, they abandoned their location in the inner city and moved to Malibu. Sample stood his ground, persuaded the board, found ways to invite and support inner-city students, and built the university into a university ranked fifteenth in the nation. An article in the April 5, 2002, issue of the *Chronicle of Higher Education* describes how he raised three gifts of $100 million or more, one of them by a phone call.[9]

Sample had prepared the leaders of USC who understood well the various types of support we needed to get the Institute off the ground. We had no alums and we had an unusual mission that would need to be explained to most potential donors. To help us, President Sample did a number of things. First, the university established a university policy that any donations to the Institute by USC alums were to be counted as a gift to USC, thereby allowing their alums a simple way to fulfill their philanthropic obligations to their alma mater.

Second, the university offered office space on campus in an academic building for our president, executive director, and assistant. Third, they would donate half-time the assistance of one of their development personnel, as well as the services of their public relations office. Finally, they offered me an endowed chair in their School of Religion which allowed me to teach two courses each fall. That appointment provided half of my salary; the other half came from the Institute.

Needless to say, we were stunned by the sincerity, generosity, and thoughtfulness of the USC offer. Once our advance team reported back to the CCS, it was agreed, after some discussion, that we would establish the Institute at USC. Los Angeles is the largest Catholic archdiocese in the United States, where, on any Sunday, Mass is celebrated in over forty languages. Geographically, it sits on the Pacific Rim and serves as a doorway to Latin America. Los Angeles is a dynamic cultural and intellectual part of the United

9. Basinger, "Other People's Money."

States. The next twenty-five years proved that we had made the right decision.

Having found, finally, a home for the Institute, I still asked myself how we would meet the daunting challenges ahead of us. After our first gathering of the CCS in the Pittsburgh airport in May 1997, one participant sent me a letter the following week saying that though he thought this project was very worthy, he was struck by how difficult, even with the match, it would be to realize. The cost, he wrote, would be enormous. Then there would be the difficulty of keeping faithful to the Institute's unique mission, noting how drastically the mission of the Ford and Rockefeller Foundations changed in a single generation. He didn't feel that enough of the members of the Commission were top scholars and recommended that whoever headed the Institute, it not be a theologian, but rather a Catholic scholar with ample experience engaging the secular intellectual world firsthand. I never forgot his concerns and advice, and told him that in a letter I wrote a week later in response.

# 3

# Establishing a Board of Trustees and an Academic Advisory Council

THE APRIL 15, 1999, progress report to the CCS covered several critically important areas. First, we singled out the prospectus as making a clear case for the nature and need of the Institute. Second, we set ourselves to the task of making the mission of the Institute understood by the wider and non-academic audience. The report described the benefits for scholars who are selected as fellows of the Institute but realized that making the nature and mission of the Institute understandable to non-academic potential donors would remain a significant challenge. Third, we needed a location, an office and someone to take care of it. The report mentioned that we rented an office in Washington, DC, led by Dr. Georgia Keightley, a professor of theology at Trinity College. The District of Columbia was also the home of our newly hired fundraiser. Fourth, we had acquired a 501(c)(3) status for the Institute with officers designated and by-laws set. We summarized the reports of the two 1998 meetings (February 13–14 and November 7) of the CCS and its five subcommittees. We added further clarifications of the Institute's scholarly focus, from which everything else flowed. Fifth, the Governance Committee had reached a high degree of consensus about the size of the governing board, the types of people to serve on it, the length of appointments, the appointment of junior and senior scholars, and the importance of themes. We discussed whether a certain theme should be set for a specific year, or whether scholars should be permitted to pursue their own research. We decided later that a blend of the two approaches would be best. Sixth, we then reported that the Academic Advisory Council should include bishops supportive of the Institute. Finally, Michael Lacey and I listed nine academic associations, including the Catholic Theological Society of America, the College Theology Society, and the National Catholic Educational Association, where we had spoken in an effort to make the mission of the Institute more widely known and drum up support.

A year earlier, some members of the CCS asked whether a residential experience on a particular campus could be just as well achieved by a virtual community of scholars using technology. Paul Caron reported on an extensive study he directed on the issue. Noting that the use of technology was expanding exponentially and its future uses and development were unpredictable, he reported that the clear consensus was still that technology cannot supplant the necessity of physical location for conducting high-level research.

A report on fundraising called for a new strategy. The year before we had contracted with a professional fundraising organization to supply us with the names of individuals who might contribute as much as $5 or $10 million to the Institute's endowment. Members of the CCS started contacting these individuals in the fall of 1998. It soon became obvious that we needed to adjust our strategy, including broadening the base of support, seeking not only major gifts but also smaller ones, and contacting other foundations. We also needed to work at winning the support of the presidents of Catholic colleges and universities. We needed to hire a full-time fundraiser. In addition we needed to work carefully with members of the hierarchy to gain their public support.

Given the localism that constricted the vision of Catholic colleges and universities, it would prove difficult to get the support of their presidents. Working with foundations was both laborious and time consuming because foundations require extensive reporting including progress reports, setting outcomes, and submitting final results. Scholars who seek funding from foundations find these requirements as time consuming as actually doing the research and reporting the results. Scholars needed no convincing. They would be delighted with Abraham Flexner's Institute for Advanced Study that required of its fellows "the unobstructed pursuit of useless knowledge."

In 1999, we also began with a small group serving as the Institute's Board of Trustees. It included Paul Caron, retired from J. P. Morgan in Europe; Michael Lacey of the Woodrow Wilson Center in DC; John Noonan, US Court of Appeals for the Ninth Circuit; and Francis Oakley, the former president of Williams College. We met in person several times a year, but more often made use of conference calls. In 2001, we added two members: generous donors Arogyaswami Paulraj, the chairman/CTO of Iospan Wireless and professor at Stanford University, and James Duffy, a graduate of Princeton and Harvard Law, a retired attorney with a background in finance and banking, and also a novelist. Finally, through Kevin Starr, USC professor and California State Librarian, we began to build our relationship with USC, which was soon to become the home of the Institute. As a group, these individuals helped us navigate through the turbulent early years of the Institute until 2004 when the board came to grips with a fundamental question: whether and how to continue. That story will be told once we look at what happened between 2000 and 2004.

## THE ACADEMIC ADVISORY COUNCIL

In the 1999 progress report, the Governance Committee recommended the formation of an academic advisory council composed of distinguished scholars who could be consulted regularly for advice about issues that they thought were most important for the Catholic Church to address. Over the next year, a group of fourteen scholars accepted invitations to become members of the Academic Advisory Council, including anthropologist Mary Douglas of

London, England; philosopher Dagfinn Føllesdal of Stanford University; Cathleen Kaveny, professor of law and theology at Notre Dame; theologian Bernard McGinn of the University of Chicago; Michael Novak of the American Enterprise Institute; Archbishop Daniel Pilarczyk of Cincinnati; and philosopher Charles Taylor of McGill University.

In preparation for their first meeting, each of them was asked to write a two-page statement describing what they thought were the most critical issues facing the Church. Their responses were grouped under four broad headings: Globalization and Religious Pluralism, the Church in Relationship to Culture, the Church and Life Within It, and the Church and Science. What follows is a brief summary of the conclusions of these discussions.

Under the first topic of Globalization and Religious Pluralism, the problem of relativism has become more acute, especially in the more affluent West. There, instead of absolutes, personal taste determines much of what is considered right and wrong. The movement toward relativism, however, did not take place overnight. Its roots can be traced back to the breakup of Christendom in the late medieval period, followed by its fragmentation into national states which, in the seventeenth and eighteenth centuries, adopted either Catholic or Protestant versions of Christianity. Then came the Enlightenment which moved to privatize religion and change matters of faith understood intellectually within a community into personal matters of morality for individuals. There were also positive developments in the modern era, such as greater sensitivity to individual human experience, human rights, and individual freedom.

The powerful impact of globalization is ambiguous. While it is often seen as positive in the Western world, in most parts of the world it is experienced as a superpower's expansion of capitalistic hegemony. Popular American TV shows (e.g., *M\*A\*S\*H*, *Dallas*, and *Baywatch*) and movies (e.g., *Rambo*, *Wall Street*, and *Mission Impossible*) are viewed now nearly all over the world. News outlets present highly selective takes on "world news." On a more positive note, some Church-related universities and colleges in recent years are ahead of their secular counterparts in analyzing from ethical and theological points of view the ambiguous cultural, economic, and religious developments. Most secular universities lack a common set of ethical and religious assumptions from which to provide such an analysis.

The Academic Advisory Council members' discussion on the Church in Relationship to Culture emphasized the role of the Institute in helping the larger Church revitalize Catholic presence in influential cultural centers, a presence that is neither Constantinian nor sectarian, not a haven for conservatives or liberals, but a robust and positive renewal of the great Catholic tradition. There should be no naïveté in all this since we face in the culture a battle between life and death; at the same time, it is necessary to foster life with a sophistication that in no way dilutes the power of the gospel but will transcend the sharp right/left template that shapes so many discussions—political, ecclesial, and theological. They also advised that it would be important that the research of the Institute assist bishops and address pastoral needs. A focus must also be kept on how religion is lived by ordinary believers. Catholic theologians and academics, in general, need to pay greater attention to the growing diversity of the US Catholic population, especially Hispanics. Academics, it should be admitted, typically run the risk of narrowing their audience to people like themselves, who really constitute another minority of the population.

Finally, the dialogue between faith and culture remains multifaceted, complex, and necessary. Serious and open interreligious dialogues began only in the last one hundred years. In short, the Catholic approach to its dialogue with culture needs to be both more positive and discerning than it has been in the past.

The third topic, the Church and Life Within It, noted that we have not only a crisis in the priesthood but also in episcopal leadership. Priests and bishops need not only support but also a stronger intellectual and spiritual formation which can be fostered by the Institute in various ways. In academe, the spiritual and the intellectual realms have been severed just as in our culture "spirituality" is severed from religion with its communal institutional practices.

Academics tend to be obsessive about power, and in their research focus on power relationships. For example, an academic sociology of the Church typically eclipses the intellectual and mystical and focuses only on the institutional. Some theologians do the same. The Institute needs to develop a more complex approach to the study of Catholicism, one that, mentioned several times by the members of the Academic Advisory Council, will transcend the sterile polarizations between the left and the right. We need, the council recommended, a more accurate appropriation of tradition: for example, only fifty years ago the typical history of medieval spirituality listed practically no women authors. Most women whom we now see as important contributors to medieval spirituality were virtually unknown only a few decades ago.

The final topic, the Church and Science, noted that in the West the relationship between science and religion never hardened until the eighteenth century. Before then, from the fifteenth through the seventeenth centuries, it was more creative and fluid. When the Church and Science were deeply influenced by Greek thought, Church leaders and scientists made claims of absolute truth. Today, however, science typically sees reality in theory and models, whereas theology, for example, should focus less on theory and more on the lived experience of believers. Contemporary science depends greatly on various technologies that actually reconstruct us, the observers. Scientific discoveries and technological capabilities have forced us to ask ourselves whether we can build biological material with consciousness. If we can, then we will be forced to ask what differences there are between human and non-human consciousness. The neurosciences remain areas of critical importance for theologians and philosophers to think through the nature of the human person. Certain forms of Protestantism, particularly those best described as fundamentalistic, are drawn to science because they want proof and certainty in matters of theology and life. The Catholic tradition can offer a more sophisticated hermeneutical tradition that will take us beyond a hyper-objectivism (scientism) on the one hand, and a subjectivism (some extreme forms of postmodernism) on the other. This first meeting of the council lasted four hours. The intellectual energy and interest remained at a high level for the entire time.

On January 23, 2003, the members of the council met a second time in Los Angeles. Michael Lacey and Fr. Joseph Komonchak chaired the meeting. Among the attendees were two archbishops—Daniel Pilarczyk of Cincinnati and Oscar Lipscomb of Mobile, Alabama—along with Dagfinn Føllesdal and Michael Novak. The discussion explored three topics: faith and current culture, the sexual abuse crisis, and suggestions for important research areas for the Institute to pursue. Once again, the discussion was lively.

The members of the council read Charles Taylor's book *The Varieties of Religion Today*. Taylor argued that the primary obstacle to belief today is not epistemological but moral and spiritual, or as John Henry Newman believed, an atrophied imagination.[1] The key problem today is not the relationship between Church and State, as it was for Catholics in the United States in the nineteenth century, but between the individual and the community. Pascal's wager is not a wise way to make up one's mind about religious belief: decide that God exists and live accordingly—if you are wrong, you lose nothing. Citing Newman again, the act of faith is better understood as a convergence of probabilities.[2] One member (who did not attend this meeting) criticized Taylor for his "autobiographical secrecy," saying that he ought to be more explicit about his Catholic faith. In response, another member, defending Taylor's approach, pointed out that there was a good precedent for the indirect method of communicating the faith; namely, Thomas Aquinas's *Summa Contra Gentiles*, in which Thomas avoided explicit statements of his Christian faith so that he might speak philosophically to unbelievers with the hope that they might be led to faith.

During the discussion of the sexual abuse crisis, the members of the council agreed that different dimensions should be

---

1. Newman, *Grammar*, 321.

2. Newman to William Samuel Lilly, December 7, 1882, in *Letters and Diaries, Vol. 30*, 159–60.

distinguished: religious (sin and grace), psychological (formation and celibacy), and sociological (how widespread is the abuse?). Also agreed upon was the need to critique the culture of the hierarchy, often characterized by secrecy. There is a need for greater co-responsibility, bishops who consult more, are financially accountable, and realize that they and the entire Church are at the same time holy and sinful. Archbishop Pilarczyk said that pedophilia and homosexuality should not be lumped together and added that there is more than one clerical culture. Both archbishops realized that the 2002 Dallas Charter that addressed sexual abuse in the Church had left many priests feeling defenseless and demoralized. Very large dioceses, Pilarczyk said, are nearly impossible to govern, with the consequence that some bishops become "barons" and lose touch with the daily experiences of their priests and people.

Archbishop Lipscomb reminded the group that when it comes to fiscal accountability, there are strict guidelines for diocesan finance councils that forbid a bishop to do certain things without the concurrence of the council. To which another member said that there is a growing number of young priests who, on the parish level, dismiss already formed parish councils. Other structural problems make it easier for some bishops to avoid candid give and take. Some bishops don't want to hear bad news. Academics want more intellectual leadership from their bishops while bishops want more pastoral awareness from academics. The discussion ended at that point.

The final topic, suggestions for research, encouraged exploring the culture and spirituality of the priesthood; economic structures and justice; effective forms of preaching and catechizing; interreligious dialogue, especially between Christianity and Islam, coupled with American foreign policy in the Middle East; and strengthening the Church dialogue with modern science, especially the impact of the internet and social media.

The Institute followed up on several of the recommendations of the Academic Advisory Council. Given the richness of these discussions and the many topics they covered, we were able to commission research and publication on only a few of them.

# 4

# Competition or Complementarity?

THE REPRESENTATIVE OF THE foundation with whom we worked directly frequently asked questions about other Catholic institutes that had been founded recently on Catholic campuses. He wanted to know whether they might compete with the Institute. For example, a front-page article in the *Washington Times* dated July 23, 1997, announced a $50 million cultural center in honor of Pope John Paul II.[1] It planned to feature an interactive museum and have six residential scholars to study the works of John Paul II. A member of the foundation asked whether our Institute would simply duplicate the Pope John Paul II Cultural Center to be established in Washington, DC.[2]

Two months before the appearance of the newspaper article, the leaders of the JP II Center had actually invited Michael Lacey and me to talk with them about their plans, especially about the think tank they wanted to create as part of it. In these conversations, it became very clear that our Institute and this center were very different from each other, so much so that it could not even be said to be complementary. Besides being designed as a presidential

1. Schumacher, "$50 Million Catholic Center."

2. The Pope John Paul II Cultural Center was later renamed the Saint John Paul II National Shrine.

library for a pope, the focus of their scholars was to be limited to the teachings of John Paul II. Moreover, the scholarships they were willing to offer were so modest that only members of a religious community would be able to find them adequately supportive.

In our response to the foundation's question, we reported that our research was not limited to John Paul II, would support scholars more adequately, and would emphasize interdisciplinary and interreligious research for all of Catholic higher education. It would not engage in such activities as building an interactive museum or operate art galleries or welcome tourists. It was disappointing to us that we had to travel to DC and spend time making our difference from the JP II Center clear to the foundation.

We learned that the foundation was also looking at still other initiatives being taken in the United States. We were asked to meet with the leaders of the most prominent of these initiatives: the Jesuit Institute founded at Boston College in 1993 and the Erasmus Institute founded at the University of Notre Dame in 1998. For the next several months, I corresponded and met with theologian Fr. Michael Buckley, SJ, of Boston College and historian James Turner of Notre Dame to see if there were grounds to make the case together that the three initiatives complemented but did not duplicate each other. Both the Jesuit and Erasmus Institutes were located on Catholic university campuses. The Jesuit Institute was deeply involved in developing the religiously rooted intellectual life of many of the faculty at Boston College; all its board members were members of Boston College. The Erasmus Institute worked to deepen Catholic intellectual traditions through conversation with other religious traditions and with secular scholars. It focused on the humanities and social sciences. While many of its programs served Notre Dame, it also planned conferences on other campuses throughout the United States. Finally, it organized summer programs for graduate students and young faculty.

From the outset, the Institute for Advanced Catholic Studies aimed to be international, locate itself on a secular campus to be of service to all of Catholic higher education, be incorporated as a 501(c)(3) organization with its own lay board of trustees, and would support only scholars, some from other religions, to live together in residence so that they might explore issues important to the Catholic Church and society. It took considerable time in 1999 for the leaders of these three important Catholic research initiatives to draft a statement that all three agreed upon. We submitted our report in 1999 to members of the foundation with confidence that their support for the Institute for Advanced Catholic Studies would remain firm.

There were, however, two additional indications that the foundation's board continued to have concerns about our project. First, already in 1998, they wondered whether the existing institutes for advanced studies were really that effective. Second, two years later, they continued to worry that existing research institutes in the United States were actually duplicative and not complementary. Their worries were beginning to worry us.

In the late summer of 1998, the representative of the foundation sent a letter to us asking two questions: first, was there any way to measure the impact of existing institutes for advanced study, and second, whether the fact that no major ones have been established in the United States in recent decades is any cause for concern vis-à-vis the aims of the Institute. Michael Lacey wrote the response to these questions. He explained that while there are no formal studies on the impact of the established institutes, there are three kinds of evidence that permit people to make inferences about the degree to which these established institutions meet their objectives.

Before describing the evidence, he noted two things. First, that research-oriented foundations, both private and governmental, take for granted the efficiency that these research institutions have by supporting state-of-the-art basic research and writing by scholars in their chosen areas of concentration. It was not laziness on the part of the institutions but respect for institutional specialization. His second preliminary observation was that there were formidable obstacles to conducting a scientifically valid, empirically oriented study of influence. A study was proposed to measure the influence of the Center for Advanced Study in the Behavioral

Sciences, but was ultimately rejected due to prohibitive costs (well over a million dollars), the necessarily lengthy lifespan of such a project, and finally, the low likelihood of finding any really counter-intuitive results.

The directors of the existing centers for research also had no serious doubt about the long-term influence of the work they supported. They saw the extraordinarily high number of published books. There was also the testimony of the scholars themselves. Before leaving their year at the various institutions, these scholars were debriefed. By far the most common response of the scholars was an enthusiastic endorsement of the experience which they affirmed had been deeply influential in their own lives as thinkers and writers. All the existing institutes regularly conduct rigorous evaluations of their efficiency, often by commissioning a survey conducted by independent research teams. Lacey concluded his response by underlining the formidable challenges the Institute for Advanced Catholic Studies faced in getting established. He feared that a combination of inertia, deep-seated localism, and a historic indifference, if not hostility, to the claims of research scholarship on the part of our clerical leadership and the Catholic Church would prevail.

Two years later, the second question posed by the foundation was whether existing Catholic research institutes already meet the needs that the Institute for Advanced Catholic Studies is designed to meet. The foundation asked a Jesuit at Georgetown University to do his own evaluation of the four existing Catholic institutes: the Erasmus Institute at Notre Dame, the Lumen Christi Institute in Chicago, the Jesuit Institute at Boston College, and our project. He called the directors of all four of the institutes. During my phone interview with him, I asked him to speak with three members of the Institute's board.

In his report, he gave little weight to the problem of localism, despite the three-page essay written by Notre Dame historian and member of the original CCS Philip Gleason. He documents clearly the deleterious effects of competition between Catholic colleges and universities, even between those founded by the same religious order. At Stanford, Jesuit Fr. William P. Leahy wrote a study of Jesuit higher education. He became president of one of the major Jesuit universities. One chapter of his dissertation, later published as a book, described the inability of the presidents of Jesuit universities and their provincials to collaborate in the 1930s to meet a major need: the creation of a single, credible graduate school program at one of the Jesuit schools supported by all the other Jesuit universities.[3] It went nowhere. Each of the presidents and their respective provincials viewed such collaboration as a diminishment of their freedom to build their own universities. Such localism is one of the main reasons why the leaders of the IACS chose to not be at a Catholic university.

Other misrepresentations of the Georgetown Jesuit's report included his assumption that we would allow only Catholic scholars to benefit from our Institute. He also expressed his opinion that the quality of the work done by scholars at the Institute would unlikely be reliably better than what Catholic scholars at Catholic universities already produce. He overlooked that the impact that living together with other scholars for a full academic year without teaching responsibilities, departmental meetings, and committee responsibilities has been repeatedly shown to be one of the major benefits of institutes for advanced studies. Perhaps most baffling to me, he claimed that our institute was deeply influenced by presuppositions characteristic of research universities of the 1950s and 1960s. He never explained why he thought this. What the Institute was and is about is something very different from the mission of secular research universities. The Institute stresses both faith and reason, the importance of both the intellectual and the spiritual lives, and the desire to enrich not only the academy, but also the Church and society.

The consultant's final remark dismissed the vision and impact of the Institute. He reported that the type of faculty who would be most interested in the Institute would come from mid-level Catholic universities, institutions with less experience and with fewer resources. He thought that the top-tier Catholic universities

---

3. Leahy, *Adapting*.

already provided sufficient research opportunities for their faculty. In short, the leading Catholic colleges and universities had no need of the services of the Institute, but it could provide remedial help to B-level universities and colleges. He described the Institute as providing sabbaticals for mediocre scholars, adding that major Catholic universities were already doing that. After all these comments that undermined the importance and mission of the Institute, he ended his report with what might be described as slight praise:

> Over time it [the Institute for Advanced Catholic Studies] may grow into one mature research institute as envisioned by its founders, but it should not be judged a failure if it does not achieve [its goals] in the short and medium term since a quick review of the other institutes for advanced studies will show that they at their origins trod much the same gradual path to excellence.

This report was submitted directly to the foundation that planned to fund the Institute project. It may well have weakened the foundation's support of the Institute project, especially since it obscured the distinctiveness of the Institute project. In a word, the report was hardly an endorsement. We soon discovered that the foundation's concerns about duplication of existing institutions were not the only things we had to worry about. Once the conservative Catholic press got wind of what we planned to do, we had to defend ourselves on another front: some members of the hierarchy.

# 5

# Criticism and Controversy

ALREADY IN EARLY 1998, we had sent letters to all the archbishops and cardinals in the United States explaining our intention to establish the Institute and outlining its mission. Only a few bishops responded, one even with a $5,000 check in support of our efforts and structure. That bishop was Gregory Aymond, whom I had met at several National Catholic Educational Association meetings at which I had spoken. In 1998 he was the Auxiliary Bishop of New Orleans and then became the Archbishop of New Orleans in 2009. We anticipated that some bishops would not support an institute that claimed to be juridically independent of direct episcopal control and still claim to be Catholic. Other bishops thought that our plan to locate the Institute at a non-Catholic university with a lay board of trustees would only make it easier for scholars to oppose the teachings of the Church. Some of these bishops had difficulty understanding that Pope John Paul II's 1990 apostolic constitution on Catholic higher education, *Ex Corde Ecclesiae*, had already recognized the autonomy of a Catholic university and its "academic freedom rightly understood," especially in the United States where lay boards of trustees held fiduciary responsibility. These bishops had difficulty grasping the encyclical's limitations of their juridical authority. In short, with regard to Catholic colleges and universities with lay boards of trustees, bishops had to learn that while they did not have the authority to hire or fire professors, they did retain the right to determine whether individual scholars or the institution as a whole could legitimately claim to be Catholic.

The first attack was launched by the *National Catholic Register* in a front-page article titled "Academic Institute to Sidestep Bishops," which appeared in the spring of 1999.[1] On March 5, 1999, ZENIT, a Rome-based news agency run by the Legionaries of Christ, quoted with alarm one of our statements: the Institute "will enjoy the support and encouragement of the American hierarchy, but not be jurisdictionally related to them." The article also quoted Fr. Matthew Lamb, originally a Cistercian but later a diocesan priest and professor of theology at Boston College, who told ZENIT that "given some of the views of some of the scholars on the Commission [on Catholic Scholarship], I'm afraid the projected institute might just give some dissenters another platform to oppose the Church's papal and episcopal magisterium."[2] The following week, a lengthy editorial in the pages of the *Register* asked, "Why is a leading figure in the *Ex corde Ecclesiae* debate, a representative of Catholic universities, taking such a step? Why are efforts being made to create such an institute not 'jurisdictionally related to' the bishops?"[3] At that time, I was chair of the board of the Association of Catholic Colleges and Universities. The reasons for our location that we had already given were obviously not credible to the people running the *National Catholic Register*, the editors of ZENIT, or Fr. Matthew Lamb.

---

1. Caulfield, "Academic Institute to Sidestep Bishops." The *Register* was founded in 1927 as the national edition of the *Denver Catholic Register*. On August 6, 1970, Patrick Frawley's Twin Circle Publishing Co. purchased the financially struggling *National Catholic Register*, changing its editorial focus from progressive to conservative. In 1995, Frawley sold the paper to Circle Media, a ministry of the Legionaries of Christ. Eternal Word Television Network acquired the paper in 2011 from the Legionaries of Christ. The *Register*'s current owner is the Eternal Word Television Network, Inc. of Irondale, Alabama, which also owns the Catholic News Agency.

2. Caulfield, "Academic Institute to Sidestep Bishops."

3. Editorial, *National Catholic Register*, Apr. 4–10, 1999, 8.

In 1999, the final version of the implementation of Pope John Paul II's 1990 encyclical was about to be published, including the Vatican's request that all theologians teaching Catholic theology ask their local bishop for a mandatum indicating his or her orthodoxy, and that at least 50 percent of the faculty be Catholic. At that same time, two presidents of major Catholic universities published an article in *America* that predicted almost catastrophic consequences to Catholic higher education if the mandatum became a requirement.[4] I was invited by the *Chronicle of Higher Education*, a secular journal for all colleges and universities in the United States, to offer a response. They published it as "Have Catholic Colleges Reached an Impasse?"[5] I did not describe our situation as an impasse. Rather, I described it as a point of tension about a substantive matter that I was confident would be worked out. Given the *National Catholic Register's* article, their editorial, the *America* magazine article, and the imminent approval by the Vatican of a final version of the implementation of *Ex Corde Ecclesiae*, there was a very tense atmosphere for Catholic higher education in the United States that made the acceptance and support of the Institute harder to gain. Moreover, responding to these attacks once again consumed precious time.

When the news of the Institute's first full-time fundraiser was announced, these same newspapers and individuals added more fuel to the fire. Upon learning that the fundraiser was a member of the Sovereign Military Order of Malta and a member of the Equestrian Order of the Holy Sepulchre, these critics questioned how such an outstanding Catholic would work for an institute that "rejects any jurisdictional authority of the magisterium."[6]

Once again, we had to defend and explain the mission of the Institute. We had already sent out letters about the Institute to all the US cardinals, archbishops, and bishops, as well as to many presidents of Catholic colleges and universities explaining the Institute. Now, we decided that it was time for another careful

4. Monan and Malloy, "*Ex Corde Ecclesiae*," 6–12.
5. Heft, "Catholic Colleges," 89–90.
6. Cosgrove, "Academic Institute," 1.

public statement at greater length. Judge John Noonan agreed to give what would be our first major public explanation and defense of the Institute. He did so in the form of an address given on May 9, 2000, at Harvard. It was published in the July 1–8, 2000, issue of *America* magazine (see appendix E). In his address, Noonan explained that "Catholicism cannot be studied as a fossil," and "such an institute is appropriately the work of believers."[7] Commenting on Noonan's address, the editors of *Commonweal* explained that "although eager for the support and counsel of the hierarchy, the Institute would be independent of any direct clerical supervision." They added that "it would also be good if the IACS broadened its mandate to include outstanding contributions from Catholics in the arts, the media, the professions and elsewhere. Intellectual culture, even expressly Catholic intellectual culture, cannot live by scholarship alone."[8] From the earliest stages of planning, the vision of the Institute has included the arts.

Although the *Commonweal* editorial was positive, the *National Catholic Register* wrote to Archbishop of Cincinnati (the diocese in which I lived) Daniel Pilarczyk, concerned that "almost all of those who serve on the Institute's advisory board are outspoken opponents of the bishops in the *Ex corde Ecclesiae* debate." They also repeated their claim that the Institute "stands outside the jurisdiction of the necessary ecclesial authorities."[9] From 1999 on, I had kept Archbishop Pilarczyk fully informed about the Institute. He had served as the president of the United States Conference of Catholic Bishops from 1989–1992 and chaired the bishops' committee that oversaw the implementation of *Ex Corde Ecclesiae's* mandatum (the NCCB Ad Hoc Committee on the Mandatum). He wrote the following response to the *Register*:

> It is not correct to say that the Institute for Advanced Catholic Studies will be outside of Church jurisdiction. True, it will not be a university subject to *Ex corde Ecclesiae*. It will not be, or pretend to be, in any sense

7. Noonan, "Institute for Advanced Catholic Studies," 11.
8. "Something New," para. 5.
9. Brian McGuire, letter to Archbishop Pilarczyk, May 18, 2000.

a teaching authority. It will, however, be subject to the jurisdiction of the local ordinary wherever it is located. An ordinary always retains the authority to clarify what is authentically Catholic—or not—within its diocese. I endorse the Institute, I expect to continue to endorse the Institute, and I will be happy if my support is helpful. It is a wonderful project.[10]

Another member of the Catholic hierarchy Cardinal Bernard Law did not acknowledge the letter we sent to him about the Institute. I knew that he agreed with the Institute's critics (e.g., Matthew Lamb). Law had also publicly criticized the Catholic Theological Society of America. I sent a second letter to Cardinal Law about the Institute. He sent that same letter back to me with the statement, in his own handwriting, "We have nothing to talk about. BJL."[11]

Several weeks later, on a Tuesday afternoon in February of 2001, I was in my office at the University of Dayton when I received a call from Cardinal Mahony's theological advisor, Michael Downey. He said that he had received a five-page, single-spaced letter from a "highly placed ecclesiastic" advising Cardinal Mahony to revoke his letter of endorsement for the Institute (the year before we had gathered about twenty-five such endorsements and published and circulated them among leaders in the Catholic Church in the United States). I said, "Oh, Cardinal Law?" He was silent for a moment and then replied that he wasn't able to tell me who it was from. I then volunteered to tell him what I thought was in the letter. I mentioned several criticisms that I had heard from various people in the Boston area. He laughed and asked if I had a copy of the letter. He then explained that the author of the letter wanted Cardinal Mahony to revoke his public endorsement of the Institute because the author of the letter claimed that the Institute was a dangerous initiative led by a group of scholars who wanted to establish a research organization outside episcopal control. Downey had a meeting with Cardinal Mahony on Thursday

10. Archbishop Pilarczyk, letter to Brian McGuire, June 8, 2000.
11. Cardinal Bernard Law, letter to author.

of that week and asked me to provide him with more background information on the Institute so that his advice to Mahony could be more informed. He said he would call me back after the meeting on Thursday to inform me of Mahony's decision. He did call back that Thursday afternoon and let me know that Mahony would stand by the Institute. Mahony refused to revoke his endorsement. I was relieved.

On Monday, March 26, 2001, Archbishop Daniel Pilarczyk called me. I was again at my desk at the University of Dayton. He told me that he had just received a fax from Cardinal Josef Ratzinger, the head of the then-called Congregation for the Doctrine of the Faith. Ratzinger asked him three questions: "What is your opinion of the Institute for Advanced Catholic Studies? What do you think its impact will be on Catholic Theology? And, what do you think of Fr. James L. Heft, SM?" Pilarczyk then said to me, "You answer the first two questions in no more than two pages that I can edit as I see fit. You can also suggest something as an answer to the third question. Send your answers to me in the next two days." I did so (see appendix F). He edited the answers to all three questions and faxed them back to Cardinal Ratzinger, endorsing the Institute even more strongly than what I had suggested to him. (Unfortunately, I have been unable to find that text.) Within two weeks, the archbishop received another fax from Ratzinger thanking him for his fax and wrote that it put things in perspective. We never heard another thing. The following year the sexual abuse explosion in Boston caused Law to resign on December 13, 2002, and move to Rome where he died on December 20, 2017.

# 6

# Conflict with Another Cardinal

ONCE IT WAS DECIDED that we would establish the Institute at USC, it became obvious that I would need to eventually leave the University of Dayton and devote myself full time to the work of establishing and building the Institute. From 2003 to 2006, however, I had been traveling twice a month to Los Angeles where I met frequently with leaders of USC (their doors remained remarkably open) and did my best to engage with more potential donors.

One of the most important challenges we had to deal with after the Cardinal Law episode was a serious misunderstanding with Cardinal Mahony. It was about fundraising and the people we were seeing for donations.

Signals of tension over money were received already in the fall of 2002. The new Cathedral of Our Lady of the Angels was consecrated in 2002; at the ceremony, the cardinal announced that it had been fully paid. The total cost was approximately $190 million. Despite that great accomplishment, the cardinal was worried about a law being prepared in the California legislature concerning sexual abuse of minors that would extend the statute of limitations for reporting sexual abuse cases.[1] The cardinal understandably

---

1. The first window of time for reporting sexual abuse in California was one year (2003). The second window was three years: January 1, 2020 to December

## Conflict with Another Cardinal

worried that the passage of such a law would generate an avalanche of new abuse claims.

In an email to me dated September 26, 2002, the cardinal expressed his delight that we had maintained a national and even international scope for our fundraising efforts. He was relieved that the national Institute would not become a Los Angeles *burden*. I should have paid more attention to that word. Although it was true that we had focused on donors located elsewhere in the United States and in Europe, he was receiving reports that we were calling on some of his best Los Angeles supporters and donors.

In an effort to keep the cardinal informed about our fundraising efforts, I sent him a long letter in October 2003 describing our national and international efforts to raise money. At the end of the letter, I also mentioned two wealthy potential donors in the Archdiocese of Los Angeles, one who had contributed substantially to the building of the new Cathedral and another who was not Catholic but a close friend of the former mayor of Los Angeles, Richard Riordan. After he had received that letter, he said nothing about our fundraising and continued to be very friendly with me at various archdiocesan events that I attended. I assumed, incorrectly, that there were no misunderstandings between us on the matter of fundraising.

The cardinal's anger flashed when, late one evening, I emailed him asking his permission to contact a well-known person in Los Angeles who had helped him in his fundraising for the cathedral. I was hoping that she would become a member of the Institute's Development Committee. I thought that in an effort to be completely transparent, I would first ask his permission to contact her. Within minutes (it was after 11 p.m.), I received an email from him stating that he was becoming increasingly concerned about the Institute taking his best people to do fundraising for the Institute. He added

---

31, 2022, for victims who were previously barred from filing lawsuits due to the previous statute of limitations to file claims. In 2023, AB 452 became a new law in California that removed the time limits to file a civil lawsuit related to sexual abuse, at least as it relates to a minor.

in bold that "it won't take much more of this to turn me into a real enemy of your project." Needless to say, I was stunned.

Several days later, I learned that Mahony had sent a three-page letter to my provincial, Bro. Stephen Glodek, SM, stating that I had greatly misled him about the fundraising that I was doing locally and that, as a consequence, he was withdrawing his support for locating the Institute in Los Angeles. He claimed that we had told him that 95 percent of the funding would come from outside Los Angeles. He wanted the Institute out of his archdiocese and located at some Catholic university elsewhere in the United States. He added that some of his contacts in Los Angeles were also concerned about the Catholicity of our research, about some of our programs, and my own orthodoxy. The cardinal's letter put the Institute's future in serious doubt. The danger that he would speak publicly against it would complicate all of our funding efforts, not just those in Los Angeles. At that time, the decision to locate the Institute at USC had already been made but I had not yet left Dayton and taken up permanent residence in Los Angeles.

Upon receiving the letter, my provincial called and informed me about its content (at that time I did not have a copy of it). After some discussion, I suggested that it would be best if he would send a letter to the cardinal informing him that while the Marianists remained supportive of the project and were confident about the Institute's and my orthodoxy, the Institute was not a Marianist-sponsored work. He agreed to do this. I drafted the letter and emailed it to him. In that letter, Glodek explained that I reported to a lay board of trustees, and that the Institute was therefore not under the jurisdiction of the Marianists. In effect, Bro. Glodek suggested, as I had recommended, that the cardinal discuss his concerns with the Institute's board. The cardinal agreed to a meeting with leaders of the board.

It took several months to put together an international committee of three of the board members for this important meeting. In the meantime, shortly after my provincial forwarded to me a copy of the cardinal's letter, I sent the cardinal a hand-written letter explaining that we continued to work hard to raise money

## Conflict with Another Cardinal

nationally and internationally and that locally we have worked mainly with alumni of USC who wanted to support the Institute. I also apologized for contributing to any misunderstanding.

Several months before this flare up, I had planned a trip to Rome. For several years I had been visiting the Vatican annually to update various cardinals there about the Institute. I gave them copies of the books we had published, and kept them informed about our mission and research plans. The board encouraged these visits because they realized that the idea of locating a Catholic research institute at a secular university without direct juridical supervision by a bishop was very unusual or, in contemporary argot, "outside the ecclesiastical box."

A European member of our Academic Advisory Council and a major donor, Mr. Ernesto Rossi of the Rossi/Martini family, heard about my conflict with the cardinal. He suggested that I should meet again with a friend of his who at the time was serving the Pope (John Paul II) in an important capacity. John Paul II had appointed Rossi's close friend, Cardinal Georges Cottier, OP, as his theological advisor, a role traditionally reserved since the Protestant Reformation for a Dominican theologian. Most popes are not theologians and benefit from regular expert advice on theological matters.

Already in June of 2000, three years before this conflict with Cardinal Mahony, Rossi had arranged for a conversation for me with Cardinal Cottier about the Institute. Both Rossi and I met then with Cardinal Cottier. I was honored to meet with him.

We shared some of the Institute's literature, including the prospectus. The cardinal was very supportive and offered several comments about the mission of the Institute. First, he said that there was an urgent need for a deeper Catholic intellectual sensibility among scholars. Second, he encouraged us to acquire some endorsements from some cardinals (ironically, we already had Cardinal Mahony's endorsement which Cardinal Law wanted him to revoke). Third, as a good Dominican, he hoped the Institute would support both a spiritual as well as an intellectual formation for scholars. He recalled a saying popular among Dominicans: First the bow is bent in study, then the arrow is released in preaching.

This time, my meeting was not about the idea of the Institute, but about a crisis that exploded between Cardinal Mahony and the Institute over fundraising. Rossi had arranged for me to meet with Cottier alone in his Vatican office. He spoke in French and I in English. We understood each other well. During the conversation, it became evident that he continued to support the Institute. He was no stranger to various disputes and disagreements among cardinals. After about twenty minutes, he asked to be excused for a moment. He returned with a letter typed on papal stationery signed by himself. In it, he made clear his strong support for the Institute and for my vision of its mission. He said that I could use the letter, even make it public if that would be helpful. I had tears in my eyes. I never did use it.

After discussing the current crisis with members of the Institute's board, we decided that it would be best if three members of the board met with the cardinal to clarify the fundraising goals of the Institute and address the concerns he had raised in his letter to my provincial. In the meantime, I laid low. The board selected three of its members to be the Institute's delegation: Francis Oakley, Jill Ker Conway, and Paul Caron.[2]

They met with the cardinal on March 31, 2004. The meeting, scheduled for thirty minutes, lasted nearly an hour. A summary of that meeting drawn up afterward indicated that "the atmosphere was fine. The cardinal was firm but courteous, and we in turn, were appropriately polite but not supine." The minutes described the cardinal's style as a mixture of "condescension and diplomacy." A week before the meeting, we had sent to the cardinal a description of the three-member committee. Surprisingly, at the beginning of the meeting, the cardinal said that members of a board of a research institute could not be expected to have any real experience

2. At the time, Francis Oakley was the former president of Williams College and a historian of ideas. Jill Ker Conway's background was described in footnote 5, p. 25. Paul Caron was responsible for J. P. Morgan's international business in Europe, the Middle East and served on the boards for a number of West Coast and New York based multinationals in Europe.

in the gritty business of fundraising. In response, the Institute's delegation did their best to "disabuse him of that notion."

Six weeks later, the committee sent the cardinal their understanding of the agreements they had reached in their meeting with him. He approved the summary with only minor changes. The agreement indicated that the Institute understood that it did not figure institutionally among the archdiocese's formal fundraising priorities; that the Institute's financial strategy remained focused primarily on national and international sources; that alums of USC who wanted to give to the Institute would pose no problem; that donations from non-Catholics in Los Angeles would be fine as well as unsolicited donations from Catholics in Los Angeles; and that the cardinal would continue to speak positively of the Institute. The cardinal also agreed that we could continue to publicize his endorsement of the Institute and use his photo in our literature. Finally, the Institute agreed to keep a delegate of the cardinal informed about any major Institute events in the Archdiocese. The cardinal also agreed to meet at some point in the future with all the members of the board to affirm the agreements reached at the March meeting.

Because of the skill of our board delegation in meeting with the cardinal, a major crisis was averted. We did not have another conflict with the cardinal who later became very supportive of the Institute. For example, in May 2010, the cardinal sent a handwritten note to me after attending an Institute event at USC that celebrated its history and accomplishments. He wrote, "A great event last night! You have created something really extraordinary for the Church in our country! Thanks for all that you do to serve the Church with such distinction!"

The week before I had also received a letter from the newly-appointed archbishop of the Los Angeles archdiocese, José Gomez, assuring me of his prayers and support. On September 29, 2010, we arranged for Cardinal Mahony to speak at USC on "Common Ground on Immigration Reform."

In October of 2010, the Institute and the Pontifical Council for Justice and Peace co-sponsored a conference titled "*Caritas in Veritate* and the United States." The conference was held in the Vatican.[3] Several months before the conference, we asked Cardinal Mahony if he would be willing to write a letter to all of his US fellow bishops about the Vatican conference. He did. In that letter, he wrote that the Institute was one of the most important places in the Church to carry out Pope John Paul II's call for Catholic intellectuals to engage the major issues in today's society. In short, our relationship with the cardinal remained cordial and supportive, especially as he, on February 27, 2011, turned seventy-five, the age for mandatory retirement.

---

3. Two years later, Oxford University Press published our study on Pope Benedict's encyclical.

# 7

# Fundraising and Foundation Pledge Agreement

ONE OF THE MOST perplexing and difficult situations we faced was dealing with the foundation that had pledged to match every million dollars we raised until we had reached $50 million. At times, the foundation seemed solidly in support of our project and then at other times, they asked if the Institute was trying to do something that already existed. It may be the case that the representative of the foundation was always supportive of the Institute, but that the board of the foundation to which he reported, was actually raising most of the questions and seeking additional assurances that the proposed gift agreement would actually bear fruit. We never found out.

In a memo dated February 6, 1998, the representative of the foundation stated that the foundation wanted to play a strong supportive role provided two major requirements were met: (1) clear goals and methods and (2) convincing support from all key constituencies, including major Catholic universities and colleges. Very early on we tried to explain to the representative that given the localism of Catholic colleges and universities in the United States, it would be very unlikely that they would support a freestanding institute, even though the very reason we planned to locate the Institute at a secular research university was to be of service to all of Catholic higher education. We also reminded him, recalling Fr. Hesburgh's experience, that it would not be easy to raise money to support faculty research. And finally, we faced the additional difficulty of trying to raise millions of dollars for an idea that many donors had trouble understanding—namely, the critical importance of strengthening the distinctive Catholic intellectual tradition.

In May 1999, our liaison with the foundation who worked directly with us gave a very positive report to the entire board of the foundation. He spoke of the Institute as the foundation's "large project," and assured the board that the CCS, which had subdivided into five subcommittees, had been working diligently to determine many of the questions that needed to be answered to give full support to the Institute. He reminded the board that Scott Appleby of Notre Dame and I had travelled to the Netherlands and given a well-received report to the full board on December 1, 1998. He reported on the encouraging meetings we had with Cardinals Danneels and Martini, the decision made to support the hiring of a full-time fundraiser and the identification of potential major donors. Finally, he stated that while he was not assured that all the essential elements would fall in place, the Institute could address the most crucial needs of the whole system of Catholic higher education and the formation of its faculty.

Despite this positive report, the foundation board seemed concerned that the fundraising was not moving fast enough. In a memo to me, the representative of the foundation stressed the importance of hiring an excellent fundraiser who would operate on a tight timetable to make progress on meeting the target of matching grants. He wrote that there needed to be a "strong sense of urgency." In short, further work needed to be done on a step-by-step conceptual plan and credible evidence of funding support. He also indicated that we needed to address the issue of competition.

After that meeting with the board of the foundation, our liaison again made it clear that deadlines needed to be tightened, major gifts received or at least agreed to in writing, and demonstrable progress made in the following year. It was at that time that we began to look for a qualified professional fundraiser.

The Argidius Foundation generously supported the planning phase, contributing nearly a million dollars that would support the work of the CCS. Once that planning was completed, we understood that the foundation agreed to provide a maximum of $25 million for endowment purposes in a one-to-one matching grant in three stages. That is, for every million that the Institute could raise up to $10 million, the foundation would match that same amount, which would mean that the Institute would have a $20 million endowment. There would then be a second commitment by the Institute to raise an additional $10 million that the foundation would match to create a $40 million endowment. Finally, in the last stage, for every million raised by the Institute, the foundation would add an additional million up to $5 million. This would then be a total of $50 million for the endowment. The original document suggested that a deadline of three to five years ahead be set for reaching fundraising goals. If the $50 million goal was not reached within the agreed upon deadline, then the foundation would not make any of its matches. After conversation with the leaders of the CCS, it was agreed that a deadline of 2001, three years from then, would be a reasonable deadline for raising the first $10 million.

The representative of the foundation took a great, continuing, and sometimes meddlesome interest in the success of the project. We had warned him about the localism of Catholic higher education in the United States and the unique nature of the Institute, but we were also concerned about the growing polarization within the American Catholic hierarchy and the opposition we might receive from some of them.

Then, suddenly, without warning, the terms of the pledge of the foundation changed. The liaison with the foundation no longer spoke of $25 million. Instead, he started speaking of $10 million and the $5 million additional dollars possible once the $10 million match was made. Less than six months after that, the representative of the foundation spoke only of $10 million, not $10 million plus $5 million more. We were confused. What was happening? Realizing that beggars cannot be choosers, we decided not to ask. But then we realized that an informal agreement could change again or even completely disappear. We decided that we needed a formal agreement that guaranteed the original understanding between the foundation and the Institute.

On December 22, 2000, we received from the foundation a draft of a formal agreement. It stipulated that by January 1, 2001, twelve days later (!), the Institute would be required to present reasonable proof that it had raised $10 million. In addition, the agreement stipulated that the $10 million of the foundation's money would be paid to the Institute *only after* it had established to the reasonable satisfaction of the foundation that it had pledges in the amount of $25 million. If proof of the additional pledges amounting to $25 million were not raised by January 1, 2002, the foundation would not be obligated to pay any amount to the Institute.

We were stunned. The Institute's board met to discuss the foundation's proposed agreement. The December 22 proposal stated that we would receive the $10 million only once we raised the additional $15 million. We had already raised over $5 million and were working hard to raise the additional $5 million so that the foundation would give us a match of $10 million. We would then have $20 million. We had proposals out for $7 million gifts and had not yet received a no. We had good reason to believe that we could make the $10 million deadline of January 1, 2002. As recently as three months before, we had understood in conversation that the foundation was then prepared to match $10 million that the Institute would raise and subsequently an additional $5 million that the foundation would match for a total of $30 million. For several months, there had not been any mention about the foundation's original plan to match million for million up to $25 million that the Institute would raise.

We had understood that when the $10 million was raised, the foundation would simply match it without any further conditions. However, the proposed written agreement now stated that by January 1, 2002, the Institute also had to prove possession of additional pledges of $15 million. If the Institute was unable to do that, the original $10 million would be returned to the foundation which then would owe nothing more to the Institute. In short, the match was now not a match, it was only a loan. In the light of the foundation's proposed agreement, we were required to tell our current donors that their donations were not being matched by the foundation unless within a year's time we had raised a total of $25 million.

We had been put in a very difficult situation. Thinking that the board members of this European foundation did not understand well the realities of fundraising for scholarly work in the United States, we asked that we be allowed to make a presentation to the board of the foundation on May 16, 2001, to clear up misunderstandings and set, if possible, more reasonable deadlines for reaching the goal of raising the first $10 million.

On the morning of May 16, 2001, we landed in the Netherlands and met with members of the foundation's board. Our Institute board agreed that three of us would meet with them: Michael Lacey, Paul Caron, and I. In our presentation, we thanked them for their support, and then explained to them as clearly as possible the unique vision of the Institute, the challenges we faced, the fundraising successes to date (just over $5 million), and our confidence in success to meet the $10 million match during the rest of the year. We also explained what we needed from them to move forward with confidence, specifically that the deadline be extended to January 1, 2002, for reaching the $10 million match.

Later that same day, the foundation's lawyer emailed me a revised agreement that extended to January 1, 2002, the fundraising deadline to raise $10 million. However, once again, the foundation would not give us this amount permanently unless we raised an additional $10 million by July 31, 2003. If we then raised that additional $10 million, the foundation "might consider" extending the deadline once again. Obviously, we were in no position to refuse to sign the agreement. Our only option was to work as hard as we could to raise $10 million in the next nineteen months.

We did our best. We raised $7.6 million by January 1, 2002, but with only that amount, we missed the match. Any further consideration or support from the foundation ended that day. While I still do not know why the board of the foundation started to pull back on its initial promise and then refused any support once we missed the match, I can only imagine that they, a European foundation, never really grasped the special challenges that raising money in the United States to support research that would develop intellectual capital for Catholic universities posed. In retrospect, I wish we had been able to spend more time educating the foundation about those challenges.

Most of the donors understandably withdrew their donations and pledges. The person who had pledged $3 million took back his gift in order to invest it for a higher return from the market. He allowed the Institute to use that interest to continue its operations. Another donor's $100,000 gift remained with the Institute. Another $1 million donor allowed us to keep $200,000 of his gift. Given that we had enough to continue a bare-bones operation, we faced a major decision.

# 8

# Do We Persevere or Close Up Shop?

FOR THE NEXT FEW months, the Institute board members discussed whether we should continue to try to raise money or admit defeat and close up shop. Needless to say, these months were very difficult. Some board members were very discouraged. One remarked, "The Institute is an excellent and much needed initiative, but it is just not the right time for it." Others recommended strengthening the board. We still had not chosen a location but we had narrowed down the possibilities to Princeton and USC. I was asked, of course, what I thought. My own religious superiors and the University of Dayton, though supportive of the project, let me know that they would be very happy if I returned to the university.

Nevertheless, during 2002 and 2003, we decided, despite discouragement, to soldier on. We had sufficient money to cover operating costs. Those board members who remained with the initiative renewed their commitment to the mission however difficult we knew it would be to raise the money we needed to make it a reality.

In 2003, we decided to locate the Institute at USC. I was still at the University of Dayton then. Our new location meant a lot of traveling back and forth between Dayton and the West Coast. There were no direct flights from Dayton to Los Angeles. I arranged my teaching and other responsibilities at the University so that I would be free every Wednesday to Saturday so that I could travel to Los Angeles to raise money for the Institute.

Over the years, members of the board had different opinions about the best way forward. Some argued that we needed products (books published and conferences sponsored) as a way to demonstrate tangible results to donors. They believed that it was all the more important that we needed to do events that would make the mission of the Institute more visible and attractive to donors. Others argued that the fundamental mission of the Institute was the support of basic research; the products, if there were to be some, should be only books published by top scholars. With the help of the Templeton Foundation, we had already organized a one-day scholarly discussion on evolution and Catholic theology that we held on May 14, 2001, at Georgetown University. By late 2003 and early 2004, we agreed, though some reluctantly, that it would be helpful if we were able to organize some events to help with fundraising. We never lost sight of our final goal of establishing a residential center for scholars who would do basic research.

With the help of several faculty members of USC, we decided to plan an international conference at USC that we eventually named "Beyond Violence." We invited an internationally known group of six scholars, two Jews, two Catholics, and two Muslims, to explain how these three religions could and have been a source and motivation for works of justice and peacemaking. September 11 was still fresh in recent memory. Since the seventeenth and eighteenth centuries, many people have assumed that religion has caused more violence than any other force in society. They forget that Stalin, Hitler, Pol Pot, and Mao Zedong—all atheists—murdered more people in the twentieth century than any religious leaders ever did. Removing religion gives no assurance of less violence. The conference drew over two hundred people, and the papers were published by Fordham University Press with the title *Beyond Violence: Religious Sources of Social Transformation in Judaism, Christianity, and Islam.* The book continues to be used as a text in various universities, both secular and religious.

## Do We Persevere or Close Up Shop?

During the year 2004, the board began to operate with an increased level of energy. Board member Fr. J. Bryan Hehir recommended that we recruit Australian scholar Jill Ker Conway to the board of the Institute.[1] I first met Jill when she was a vice president at the University of Toronto while I was in residence there (1974–1977) writing my dissertation. I had invited her to speak at one of the meetings of the theology graduate students. She later taught at MIT and then became the president of Smith College. She accepted our invitation to join the board.

In late 2003 and early 2004, some of the board members continued to have an understandable sense of discouragement. Until we missed the match, they had worked very hard to make the Institute succeed. One of them felt we should close up shop. He sent me an email that expressed honestly his own disappointment, as well as that of two other board members. It should be quoted at length:

> I have thought a number of times over the past several months about resignation from the Board, but quashed the thought out of personal commitment to you and respect for the enormous effort you have made to keep the idea afloat. My own view is that we should have by now formally closed up the shop, and that we had a board agreement of sorts to trigger this outcome as of last fall. It is odd that in the past two conference calls no one has asked about the fate of our exit plan and its time, as I have no doubt that many have wondered about it. The silence on this point, too, is surely a sign of respect for you and what you have done. Nonetheless, I feel very queasy about our current policy of whistling through the graveyard. We could probably maintain a low level "pretend" kind of institutional existence indefinitely, but we should not do so in my opinion. It is a betrayal of our original idea. I know that USC would like us to stay, and that the fundraising climate could improve in the future. Personally, however, I do not believe any longer

---

1. Fr. J. Bryan Hehir is the secretary of Health and Social Sciences of the Archdiocese of Boston and the Parker Gilbert Montgomery Professor of the Practice of Religion and the Public Life at Harvard Kennedy School.

that even a dramatically improved climate would yield anything more than a fraction of what we need to bring the original idea to life. We are in fact not developing, but disintegrating.... I find it embarrassing to talk under these circumstances about adding new trustees, putting regional development committees into action, and convening academic advisory groups as if we had wind in our sails. We don't, and as we have learned over the past year, our advocate and protector the Cardinal is neither advocate nor protector, but at best a rather menacing watchdog. I understand the urge to keep up appearances for the good of the children and their future, but I worry that keeping up appearances is morally irresponsible. Who was it that wrote the poem about the man out in the water who, it turns out, was not waving, but actually drowning! The whole thing—the situation in the Church as a whole—is so depressing at the moment that I don't have a clear idea about what we should do. My intuition, though, is that we should be planning our own funeral, and making the event public. Some sort of public statement to the effect that we appreciate the help of all who helped and long for the day when this idea is reborn and flourishes, but for now we have done the best we can and it has not been enough. Let's toast a better future and move on. I apologize for sounding so mournful, but that is the way I feel right now. I think that you, too, would be better off to get rid of this albatross and focus on your own ministry of teaching and writing. You can make a difference there. *Cor ad cor loquitur*.[2]

It was easy to understand his disappointment. I was also discouraged. The board reluctantly recommended to accept his resignation and that of another board member. Our fundraiser resigned. A third board member also asked to resign, not because he opposed continuing, but because travel was becoming more difficult for him. He asked to be appointed to the Academic Advisory Council and to help with one of our key research projects. Two years later, another member of the board did the same—resigned—but

---

2. Email to author, late 2003.

stayed active as a member of the council. For a while, after we had missed making the match, several of us held things together hoping that soon we would find a way to move forward with the dream. We had enough money to continue operations for the next eighteenth months and were able to fund some research projects.

The decision to locate at USC became more of an advantage than we first realized. We had looked closely at a property near Princeton University, owned by the Vincentian Fathers who offered to lease it to us. We could pay the rental fees but would have next to nothing left to support staff and research projects. Only a few Princeton faculty were interested in the Institute, but the leadership of the university had no interest.

I have already described the extraordinary welcome that the president of USC, Steven Sample, and a number of other leaders of the university and of the city of Los Angeles had given us at a banquet hosted at the president's mansion. Subsequent conversations with the leadership of USC described further incentives for locating there. The space they arranged for us, at no cost, was a modest office with a reception area which several years later became an office complex with two offices, a reception room, and storage space. They also offered one of their development officers half time, along with some of the various search services that USC's Development Office could provide. Not only did they allow their alums and even some of their board members to donate to the Institute, they encouraged them to do so—an extraordinary act of generosity given how fiercely most universities guard their donors.

Despite the discouragement of the Institute's board members, others were ready to make a fresh go at it. Early in the summer of 2004, our newest board member, Jill Ker Conway, began conversations with several of these board members suggesting that a small group meet at her home in Massachusetts for an all-day brainstorming session on how to move forward, the results of which we would then share and discuss with the entire board. Two board members (Paul Caron and Francis Oakley) and I attended.

At the beginning of the meeting, I was asked to give an overview of where I thought we were and ought to go. I recalled that in 2001 we had a degree of assurance that we could make the $10 million match, and once we had raised that amount that the foundation would double it. Once we received the $20 million, we planned to find a building that we could turn into a residential center for scholars. Unfortunately, I continued, various factors converged making the fundraising difficult: the economy, misunderstandings with the foundation, opposition from some of the hierarchy, no support from Catholic universities, and only one person working full time on fundraising. It was obvious that if we were going to move ahead, we also needed to rebuild the board. I told the three board members that we should design some research projects and continue with high-profile conferences. I also said that someone else should chair the board. I stressed that we should never lose sight of our goal: building an endowment that would support a residential center where scholars could come for a year, do research, engage in conversations with each other, and develop in new and fresh ways the Catholic intellectual tradition. Having missed the match, I told them that I did not believe we were dead in the water. Instead, we needed to reconceive our situation as the building of a start-up. They agreed.

We talked at some length about the kinds of research projects that would be worth commissioning and also be attractive to donors. We decided on three research projects. The first one involved Jewish, Catholic, and Muslim scholars. I volunteered to lead this project. Then, we discussed a project on authority and tradition within the Catholic Church and, though likely controversial, still thought we should do it. Frank Oakley and, later, Michael Lacey agreed to lead this research project. Third, we agreed that we should organize a research project on Catholic social teaching and economic processes. Paul Caron agreed to lead this effort.[3] He later recruited Clifford Longley of the British Catholic journal

---

3. Paul Caron played an important role in the establishment of the Institute. At a dinner in 1998, Fr. David Toolan, SJ, introduced Paul Caron to Michael Lacey and me. By the end of that dinner, we invited Paul to join the board. He turned out to be an excellent, creative, and dynamic board member until his death from leukemia on December 19, 2013.

*The Tablet*.[4] Longley had recently helped the English bishops draft a pastoral letter on economics and the common good. Caron also recruited Dr. Daniel K. Finn, a professor of theology and Clemens Professor of Economics at St. John's University in Collegeville, Minnesota, to work on this project. The board soon invited Finn to become a member. The research project was named "True Wealth of Nations," which, to date, has produced six major studies, all edited by Daniel Finn.

All three of these projects came to fruition. In collaboration with Fr. David Burrell, CSC, and Rabbi Michael Signer, both of Notre Dame, we invited an international group of top scholars from Jewish, Catholic, and Muslim traditions to write papers. We then met for four full days at the Tantur Ecumenical Institute in Israel to discuss each other's papers. The papers had been mailed to each member two months earlier. No one read their papers to the others. They had read all of them before they arrived at Tantur. The discussions were extraordinary. Later, Oxford published the papers in a book titled *Learned Ignorance: Intellectual Humility among Jews, Christians, and Muslims*.

The first volume on Catholic social teaching and economic processes, *True Wealth of Nations: Catholic Social Thought and Economic Life*, was published by Oxford University Press in 2010. The "True Wealth of Nations" theme proceeded to unfold in a continuing series of excellent studies all devoted to economics and Catholic social teachings. Those publications caught the attention of leaders in the Vatican who, years later, invited us to organize two international conferences held in Rome. The project on tradition and authority became the *Crisis of Authority in Catholic Modernity* also published by Oxford University Press in 2011.

I also organized a lecture series held on USC's campus and invited five Catholic scholars, each of whom had spent years in

---

4. "*The Tablet* is a Catholic weekly journal that has been published continually since 1840. It reports on religion[,] current affairs, politics, social issues, literature and the arts with a special emphasis on Roman Catholicism while remaining ecumenical. It is committed to the teaching of the Second Vatican Council. . . . Since 1976, it has been owned by The Tablet Trust." https://www.thetablet.co.uk/about.

interreligious conversations with members of one of the great religious traditions, either Judaism, Islam, Hinduism, Buddhism, or Confucianism. Two scholars from each of the five religions were invited to critique the Catholic presentation regarding the current state of the interreligious dialogue with the Catholic Church and their respective religions. The Catholic scholar wrote responses to the two critiques.[5] The collection was published as *Catholicism and Interreligious Dialogue*. All of these books received excellent reviews. Other scholars have used these books in their own research and teaching.

Finally, we agreed to move forward with our second international conference, "Constructing Religious Identity in the Next Generation: Faith, Fear, and Indifference," which was held at USC October 10–11, 2004. Dr. Donald Miller, a widely published USC sociologist, and I wrote a successful $264,000 proposal that the Lilly Foundation funded. The international group of speakers included Muslims, Jews, and Christians from different parts of the world and a representative of the Pontifical Council for Culture. It was later published by Fordham University Press in 2006 and titled *Passing on the Faith: Transforming Traditions for the Next Generation of Jews, Christians, and Muslims*. A portion of the grant allowed a team of three of the scholars who participated in the conference to visit cities around the United States to describe the characteristics of "congregations that get it"—that is, churches, synagogues, and mosques that successfully passed on their religious traditions to the next generation. These conferences and publications attracted more funding, including the gradual building of an endowment that I will describe later.

An internationally known Jewish scholar, Rabbi Reuven Firestone, a specialist in Jewish/Muslim relations, wrote this about our

---

5. The scholars who participated in the interreligious dialogue presentations at USC on Catholicism and Judaism were Philip A. Cunningham, Elliot N. Dorff, Rachel Adler; on Catholicism and Islam: Daniel Madigan, SJ, Zayn Kassam, Jihad Turk; on Catholicism and Hinduism: Francis Clooney, SJ, Christopher Chapple, Swami Sarvadevananda; on Catholicism and Buddhism: James L. Fredericks, Anselm Kyongsuk Min, Huaiyu Chen; and on Catholicism and Confucianism: Peter C. Phan, Robin W. Wang, Robert Ford Campany.

conferences (he also participated in the 2003 conference, "Beyond Violence"):

> What is especially exciting about what is happening at this conference is that not only are Jews talking to one another, they are talking and sharing research and ideas with Christians and Muslims.[6]

In that same letter addressed to Jews in the United States, he wrote that the conference organized by the Institute was "one of the few authentic catalysts for real conversation between religions these days, and especially in forums where Muslims and Jews have organized together and are participating together."

All in all, the meeting organized by Jill Conway put new wind in our sails. It created a turning point in the history of the Institute. A renewed energy flowed through our subsequent board meetings. Among the new board members was Ellen Hancock who provided energetic leadership. Shortly after the meeting at Conway's home, the board appointed Ellen Hancock chair of the board. She added to the momentum. Within a month, she told me, "Jim, no one will give a $1 million gift to a part-time leader. You need to leave the University of Dayton and move to Los Angeles." I had been at Dayton for twenty-nine years as a professor, chair of a department, provost, and then an endowed university professor and chancellor. It had formed me in many ways. In all those different roles, I continued to teach at least one course every semester, not because it "kept me young" or that I wanted to be in touch with youth, but as I explained with only a little exaggeration to a faculty member, "teaching was the only source of consolation that I could count on!" For the previous four years, I had been making two trips a month to Los Angeles to meet with donors and work with the administration of USC on fundraising and preparing to make a home for the Institute at the university. This move required that I have the permission of my religious order to move to Los Angeles

---

6. Rabbi Reuven Firestone, email to author with attached letter, October 25, 2004.

and make some acceptable arrangement and understanding with the University of Dayton.

The Executive Committee of the University of Dayton's Board of Trustees worked out a separation agreement, a three-year leave. In my absence, the university would appoint someone from the faculty to fill my university professorship. If at the end of two years it appeared that the Institute had secured a viable path forward, I would resign my tenure and the university would conduct a national search to fill the position on a permanent basis. If the Institute's board decided that we should shut down the Institute, I would return in the fall of 2009. After three years away (until 2011), I would be permitted to return to the university as a faculty member in religious studies without tenure.

During my time away from the university, I was asked to continue to give a university lecture each fall (I had begun to do that in 1989 when I first became provost), conduct an overnight workshop each semester on "Hiring for Mission," and once a year offer a retreat to new faculty members. The university would offer me a $15,000 stipend each year for these services. Finally, the university asked me to sign a non-compete agreement on fundraising. In other words, while in California, I was not to ask for donations from any people already donating to the University of Dayton. This last part of the agreement disappointed me but did not surprise me. It was one more example of localism among Catholic colleges and universities that we had predicted and regularly encountered, with one notable exception that I will mention later.

In my conversations with my religious superiors, several conditions had to be met for me to be permitted to move to Los Angeles. First, they asked me to live in a religious community. (I found a home for the next six years with the Vincentian community.) They also asked that my University of Dayton salary be matched by the Institute. With the academic position given me by USC coupled with the Institute salary as president, we were able to fulfill that request. They also asked me to give them a "clear set of criteria" that would enable us to judge whether the Institute was successful for me to continue to stay in California and lead the Institute.

I think they feared that without those criteria I would remain at USC indefinitely.

Besides working out agreements with the University of Dayton and the Marianists, I also had to work out a Memorandum of Understanding (MOU) with USC. They agreed to cover half my University of Dayton salary for which I was to devote half of my time to the university. They appointed me the Alton M. Brooks Professor of Religion. I looked up who Brooks was and found that he was a Methodist minister who died in the 1920s and left money for an endowed chair. It is unlikely that he would have been happy that his donation would be supporting a Catholic priest as a professor. No one at USC ever raised an objection. The provost of the university also agreed to budget for our first year a fund of $200,000 to support Institute initiatives. The senior vice president for advancement, Dr. Alan Kreditor, who later joined the board of the Institute, would work to hire a fundraiser who would work half time for the university and half time for the Institute. Finally, the university agreed to introduce the Institute to potential donors, some of whom had generously supported the university. Any gift acquired through such an introduction would be recorded by and credited to the university, but placed at the disposal of the Institute.

I have already described the extraordinary banquet that the university president and board members held to encourage the Institute to come to USC. Once a Methodist university, founded in 1880, but now a nonreligiously affiliated private university with close to fifty thousand students, the details of this MOU document the generosity and support of USC for the Institute. After my first year at USC, I told the president that I thought the university was neither secular nor sectarian. It was not secular since it took the spiritual life seriously (they have a dean of religious life who also serves on the president's council) and that it was not sectarian since it took the study of multiple religions seriously. In 2015, the university approved a doctoral program in religious studies.

Once the decision was made late in 2004 to move the Institute to USC, discussions took place once again about where exactly to locate the Institute at the university. One possibility was the Catholic Center at USC. The property was owned by the Archdiocese, and the parish, therefore, was diocesan and headed by a diocesan priest. There had been talk for years about razing their old building and building a new campus ministry complex. They asked us if we would be interested in locating our institute offices in their new building. As we once considered the possibility of locating the Institute on the third floor of a new building for the Yale Catholic Campus Ministry, we had to sort through once again the pros and cons of locating on Archdiocesan property with a Catholic ministry focused mainly on undergraduate students. After some discussion, the leaders of the Catholic Campus Ministry (they did not call it a Newman Center) and the Institute decided against locating the Institute's offices in the about-to-be-built new Catholic Campus Ministry complex. Besides, USC had already promised to find office space for the Institute in an academic building. We were located in an office complex that has served the Institute's administrative purposes ever since.

# 9

# Going Full Time: Go West!

IN LATE JUNE OF 2006, at the age of sixty-three, I loaded a Penske rental truck with books, files, and some clothes, and drove from Dayton to Los Angeles. My older brother, a retired Delta pilot, joined me for the long ride. Think of our ride as a remake of the *Thelma and Louise* movie, but with two old guys in a truck. A new chapter in my life was about to begin: being president of the Institute full time and a chaired professor at USC. I was expected to teach two courses a year, which I taught every fall semester so that I could travel more easily in the spring and the summer.

Most of the board, but still not all, was committed to building a start-up operation. For all practical purposes, we were starting all over again, but with almost nothing. The difference of opinion on how best to move forward remained between those who wanted to focus solely on building an endowment and those who thought that to build an endowment, we needed to organize and publicize events and sponsor research projects. The endowment-focused board members believed doing projects took too much staff time and energy. They also disliked recruiting more business people to the board since they feared they would dilute the intellectual mission of the Institute. As one of them said, business people would not stimulate path-breaking intellectual work. One complained that the Institute had become more about me than about the mission.

Two of the three who resigned shortly after this discussion had been a part of the Institute for thirteen years—that is, from the very beginning. I can only be grateful for their generosity and commitment for that long and difficult time. Needless to say, I thought a lot about their criticisms of my leadership. I discussed all this at some length with several of the veteran board members and asked for their own evaluation. They continued to support me and agreed that what we most needed at this point in our history was to be better known and better funded. Business people were important for the board; publications and conferences could help with the funding.

Every year since 2007, the board set annual goals for me. First, I would give my annual report addressing the goals set the previous year. For example, in 2009 the board set five goals:

1. oversee, develop, and publish major research projects;
2. raise enough money to get through the economic downturn and focus on building an endowment;
3. create greater awareness of the Institute and its mission;
4. build the board that provides intellectual vision, advice, networking, and fundraising; and
5. manage the staff efficiently.

The following year's goals numbered four. Two goals were the same as number three and number four, along with an awareness that the economy was slowly improving. A new goal expected that, with the hiring of an associate director of research, the president would be able to delegate more responsibilities.

With the help of USC and some modestly successful fundraising, we were able to pay our operating expenses and support some fine research projects, which received very positive reviews. We were able to continue in this way relatively easily until the big economic downturn in 2008.

I believed, however, that if we were to raise money, we needed to do things that featured the richness of Catholicism as it engaged contemporary issues. We needed to continue to demonstrate in tangible ways the deep intellectual resources of Catholicism that would attract the support of smart, well-to-do, nonscholarly people. I was quite aware that many of our nonacademic donors would probably not read the books they supported financially. Since there was no Bamberger family with millions of dollars willing to support us like they did Princeton, we needed to continue on with the day-to-day efforts of engaging donors, producing solid academic resources, and continuing to build the endowment.

The leadership of the University of Dayton and my religious superiors wanted to hear from me whether I thought the Institute had a credible future. I had agreed to make that decision in 2008 so that they would have ample time to find a person to fill my position at the University of Dayton. Early in 2008, it looked as though the market would improve, or at least remain stable. We also had some indications that some donors were giving serious consideration to endowment gifts. Given these perceptions and after consulting with the board, I submitted my resignation to the University of Dayton. I gave up my tenure there. Then, all of a sudden, the market crashed in September 2008. I remember going to the chapel in the Vincentian community where I was living, and having a heart-to-heart talk with God.

Of course, fundraising became more difficult than it already was. Despite that, mainly because of the generosity of members of the board, we were able to continue to raise $350,000 to $450,000 nearly every year (2009 was the toughest) to cover salaries, expenses, and the cost of several research projects. But we had not yet raised any endowment money. The year-by-year slog had made it even more difficult for us to reach our final goal of establishing an endowment that would support scholars living in a residential center.

Although between 2009 and 2010 three of the original board members resigned, from 2007 until 2010, we were able to recruit four new board members, all of whom understood and fully realized that we were in a start-up mode. They believed that we needed to publish books and organize conferences that would engage the interest of potential donors. They also committed themselves to building an endowment.

Several events, seven to be exact, converged in 2010 that improved fundraising and strengthened the position of the Institute. First, the Vatican appointed a new Archbishop of Los Angeles, José Gomez. Cardinal Mahony, having reached the age of seventy-five, was required to submit his resignation, which the Vatican accepted. Though Gomez inherited a number of financial burdens and had a reputation of being theologically conservative, he never viewed the Institute as a financial or theological threat. At the encouragement of several members of his Theological Commission, he asked me to serve on it. It gave me an easy way to be in touch with him about important theological and pastoral questions.

Second, after twenty very successful years as president of USC, Steven B. Sample retired. The provost, Max Nikias, succeeded him. Both Sample and Nikias not only hosted dinners for our potential donors, but they also introduced us to donors, some of whom were on the university board. They did this because they were convinced of the importance of a Catholic research institute for the university, even though it was independent of USC and controlled by its own board of trustees. USC also wanted to be listed among the top ten universities in the United States. This goal required the publication of original research. During my years as president of the Institute, we published twenty books (see appendix G), a record of productivity unmatched by any other single center on campus.

Third, Notre Dame closed down the Erasmus Institute and established in its place the Notre Dame Institute for Advanced Study (NDIAS). At that time, one of our board members was from Notre Dame and conversations with him made it clear that the goals of NDIAS were quite different from the mission of the Institute. We no longer had to explain this to a foundation that worried that they would be investing in a project that duplicated what was already in existence. While the Institute and NDIAS were both committed to strengthening the Catholic intellectual tradition, interdisciplinary research, and the involvement of young and established scholars, the NDIAS was located at Notre Dame, funded by it, and served primarily Notre Dame's interests. It also became a smart way to help raise the level of scholarship at Notre Dame as well as recruit new faculty. It looked mainly eastward while IACS looked westward and southward. We purposely located ourselves at a non-Catholic university for greater independence. We were not trying to recruit faculty for any university, but sent all our scholars back to their own campus communities enriched by their time at the Institute.

Fourth, as an indication of the importance of designing and funding important research projects and conferences, the Institute's board agreed, despite the difficult economic times, to hire an associate director for research. In 2010, the Institute hired Dr. Gary J. Adler as its associate director of research. From 2010 to 2012, he worked half time for the Institute and devoted the remaining time to finishing his dissertation. He not only led research projects, but also organized the lecture series that we had initiated in 2007. In 2012, for example, he brought Dr. David Campbell, a Mormon political scientist at Notre Dame, to discuss Mitt Romney's candidacy for president. Dr. Jack Miles, a Pulitzer Prize winner, spoke on his latest book, *God in the Qur'an*, which compared portraits of Adam, Noah, Abraham, Joseph, Moses, and Jesus and his Mother as found in the Qur'an and the Old and New Testaments. In a provocative lecture, USC's Professor Sherman A. Jackson, an internationally known Muslim scholar, explained how members of the Muslim Brotherhood organization involved in the assassination of Anwar Sadat rediscovered the Qur'an while in prison and wrote pamphlets based on it opposing Muslim violence.

Adler helped design the Generations in Dialogue (GID) program (see appendix H) that brought young scholars together with an accomplished scholar in their field of academic interest for four weekends spread over a two-year period. During that time, the senior scholar mentored them in their scholarly work, strengthened them in their religious faith, and taught them how to write not just for other scholars but also for the wider public. The first GID started in July 2010 with the historian Fr. John O'Malley, SJ, as the senior scholar.

From left to right: Matthew Gaetano, PhD; Bronwen McShea, PhD; Fr. O'Malley, Anne McGinness, and John McCormack

Adler also helped organize the first of three Institute conferences held in the Vatican, the first of which was a critical analysis of Pope Benedict's social encyclical *The Moral Dynamics of Economic Life: An Extension and Critique of Caritas in Veritate*.

With Max Nikias, we were able to bring the widely acclaimed poet and literary critic Dana Gioia, a graduate of a Los Angeles Marianist high school and most recently head of the National Endowment for the Humanities, to USC as the Judge Widney Professor of Poetry and Public Culture. Adler later worked with Gioia to organize the first Catholic Literary Imagination Conference. It drew over three hundred people. The 150 high school students who visited the conference were able to meet and talk with writers whose books and essays they had read in preparation for that experience. Since then, a different Catholic university has hosted that conference every other year.

Adler also designed research programs and recruited scholars which resulted in two other publications: *Secularism, Catholicism, and the Future of Public Life: Dialogue with Ambassador Douglas W. Kmiec*, and *American Parishes: Remaking Local Catholicism*, edited by Gary J. Adler, Tricia C. Bruce, and Brian Starks. Adler served in that position for five years before moving with his wife, also an academic, and son to two tenure-track positions at Penn State. The academic work of the Institute benefitted greatly from his time with us.

Fifth, USC provided additional support to our staff by allowing us to use the interest of a $1 million USC endowment that they invested for us. For nine years, that interest helped support my assistant, Ms. Shelia Garrison, a USC graduate, who served until I stepped down as president in 2020.

Sixth, we added three new board members: Maureen Shea, the executive vice president of Right Management-Florida/Caribbean, with headquarters in Ft. Lauderdale; Julie Mork, from Denver, already deeply involved with USC affairs and who, with her husband John, was a major donor to USC; and Elizabeth Garrett, who was appointed provost of USC shortly after Max Nikias succeeded Steve Sample.[1] They all understood the nature of a start-up and strengthened the Institute with their advice, expertise, support, and generosity.

Finally, in 2010, the Marianists appointed a new provincial team. The provincial, Fr. Martin Solma, took a special interest in the Institute and eventually joined its board. He also recognized that I very much missed living with other Marianists. He decided to establish a Marianist community in Los Angeles to support the Institute and me. We searched for a home near the university, but they were all very expensive. Beth Garrett, the provost of USC and

---

1. Beth Garrett resigned from the board in the spring of 2015 to take on the presidency of Cornell University, the first woman president of that university. Before finishing her first year as president of Cornell, she tragically died of cancer.

then a member of the board of the Institute, suggested that we look at a house owned by the university and at the time occupied by five young professionals. It was located only two blocks from campus and one block from the Catholic Campus Ministry parish which was owned and operated by the archdiocese. From this location, I could easily walk to the university and no longer needed to rent an expensive parking space.

Built in 1907, the house was ideal but in need of considerable renovations. The kitchen was dysfunctional and there was only one bathroom which was also in terrible shape. Since we rented the house from USC, we had to receive permission to redo the kitchen and add two bathrooms. Another Marianist and I moved in during the summer of 2012. Over the next two years, we renovated this small, old USC rental and built at the back of the property an additional house with five bedrooms and a chapel to accommodate visitors and additional Marianists. In 2014, the first Marianist who lived with me was reassigned and the provincial then sent two men to form a Marianist community of three. For one year, two young Marianists joined us; they were studying philosophy in preparation for their seminary studies in Rome.

The next nine years together were among the happiest in my religious life. It made me remember how much I missed my religious community. We lived in the midst of the student neighborhood, which has been the custom of Marianist communities working in university ministries. When faculty learned where I was living, they often wondered why we would do that. I would kid them and reply, "Someone has to work with the pagans!" Though at times, especially on weekends, the neighborhood got loud, it was nothing that could not be handled by earplugs.

The location also made it possible for students to visit regularly. Every year I invited my students to join our community for a special dinner. I later learned that most USC students never had a professor invite them to dinner. This is customary with Marianist communities at our universities. In the back yard, we planted a garden with carrots, beans, tomatoes, and several rows of corn that startled some students who never imagined that corn could grow in the city. On the property, we also had orange, lemon, and papaya trees.

The two men the provincial picked to form our small Marianist community both happened to have been born and raised in Cleveland, Ohio. All three of us graduated from the same Marianist high school, one in 1958, another in 1961, and the last in 1965. For the three of us Midwesterners, the location, and especially the garden, gave us a small taste of Ohio. The Marianist community, with its regular prayer life and practice of hospitality, allowed me to feel like a Marianist again.

All of these changes were excellent for the Institute and certainly lifted my spirits. The relationship with the Archdiocese improved, the new leadership of USC remained supportive of the Institute, a complementary and collaborative relationship developed between the Institute and Notre Dame's Institute for Advanced Study, Gary Adler organized some excellent events and research programs, USC continued to offer support for operating expenses, and the Marianists created a wonderful support community for me. Taken together, these changes in 2010 also helped us begin to turn an important financial corner—the building of an endowment.

# 10

## Capital Campaign and Communicating the Mission

GIVEN THE 2008 ECONOMIC downturn, 2009 and 2010 were fiscally challenging. Even with USC's continuing generous support, our budget remained tight. As of November 5, 2010, we had received only $45,000 in donations. We had some reserves but still no endowment. USC was about to launch a $6 billion capital campaign and suggested we should ride that wave as best we could by starting a capital campaign of our own.

In these pages, I have frequently criticized the localism of American Catholic higher education. My own efforts to persuade the three Marianist universities to collaborate in funding a fellowship were no more successful than the efforts of the Jesuits who tried in the 1930s to pool resources to build a single, credible Jesuit graduate program in the United States. At one point, I approached the presidents of the three Marianist universities (the University of Dayton, St. Mary's University in San Antonio, and Chaminade University in Honolulu) asking if together they would be willing to fund a fellowship ($1.5 million). My proposal took into consideration their different sizes and resources. The fellowship would allow one of their faculty members each year to enjoy a sabbatical at the Institute. After some conversation, they decided they would not fund a fellowship. One of my great disappointments has been the unwillingness of the leaders of Catholic colleges and universities to contribute to building an Institute for Advanced Catholic Studies, even though they and their faculty would then have access to an environment for research that the typical sabbatical hardly matches.

There was, however, an important exception to this localism. In 2011, I received word from the president of DePaul University in Chicago, Fr. Dennis H. Holtschneider, CM, that DePaul University was donating $1.5 million to the Institute to endow a fellowship.[1] When I first came full time to Los Angeles in 2006, I lived with a community of Vincentian priests until 2012. Fr. Holtschneider often visited DePaul alumni in the Los Angeles area and stayed with the community in which I was living. During those visits, we spent considerable time talking about the state of Catholic higher education and the mission of the Institute. He understood the importance of what the Institute could do for all of Catholic higher education and showed it with the DePaul Fellowship. Several years later, he accepted our invitation to join the Institute's board and eventually chaired the board for several years.

Then, out of the blue, a member of the board and her husband came to my office and gave me a check for $1 million. I was stunned. They had set aside that amount for another purpose but changed their minds and gave it to the Institute instead. We decided to turn it into a fellowship bearing President Sample's name. (see appendix I for a description of a $1.5 million fellowship.) We received $150,000 from Rabbi Uri Herscher, the president of the Skirball Cultural Center in Los Angeles, as well as enjoying the support of other members of the Jewish community. Stanley Gold, also a Jew and a member of USC's Board of Trustees, also became a generous donor and helped us raise additional money. The board had already agreed that we would not use the interest of any endowment for operations, but instead applied it to the principal so that the endowment would continue to grow. For the first time,

---

1. The initials CM stand for the Congregation of the Mission, the Vincentians.

the Institute had an endowment of over $2 million. We were able to endow a second and then a third fellowship. Finally, what we had been hoping for, for nearly twenty years, began to become real.

It was also during these years that we undertook several other important projects. However, we never took our eye off the goal of building the endowment, especially now that we were experiencing a few successes. USC's success in fundraising moved more of the board members to believe that we, too, should consider launching a campaign. The board set a goal of building the endowment to $10 million before going public with a campaign in 2014. To help us reach that goal, President Nikias hosted dinners for Institute donors from 2012 to 2014. The support of USC remained unflagging. Having set the tentative date of 2014 to go public with the campaign for the Institute, the board worked hard to raise $10 million by then. The board also spent a lot of time discussing not just whom to seek out for major gifts, but also how to describe just what the $10 million would support. We listed three endowed fellowships to support especially accomplished senior scholars who would serve as mentors, and then senior and junior scholars, creating a kind of nine-month trialogue among these scholars that would together shape and support intellectual work that deepened the Catholic intellectual tradition. We also wanted to endow the presidency of the Institute along with a chaplaincy, convinced that both the academic and spiritual lives of scholars have for too long existed apart from each other.

During this time, we organized the second GID program that began in 2013 under the leadership of Dr. Bernard McGinn of the University of Chicago, a world-recognized historian of Christian spirituality. The Institute believed in creating mentorship opportunities for young scholars. We made it a point to bring together young and more seasoned scholars so that a dialogue with an older scholar—that is, between generations—could refresh both generations. A third GID program was led by senior scholar Gregory Wolfe, then writer-in-residence at Seattle Pacific University and the editor of the journal *Image*, on the topic of Catholic literature and writing. Exit interviews with the participants in these GID

## Capital Campaign and Communicating the Mission

programs documented how helpful they had been for them, despite the fact that they were brought together with the senior scholar for only four weekends. We made it possible for potential donors to meet with the young scholars to share their enthusiasm, and asked the donors to imagine how much richer and far-reaching, intellectually and spiritually, would be living together in such a community for nine months instead of meeting for four weekends spread over two years.

By the spring of 2014, however, we had to face that while we had had some success in building the endowment, we fell far short of the $10 million in gifts and pledges that we believed we needed to go public with a campaign. After consulting with the staff, members of the board, and fundraising veterans at USC, I wrote a memo dated January 6, 2014, explaining why it was necessary to postpone the campaign. While disappointing, we hunkered down and once again pushed ahead with even greater determination to continue to build the endowment.

Meanwhile, by 2017, two years before the end of their campaign, USC had already raised $6 billion and was looking to extend the campaign for four more years, this time with the goal of raising $10 billion. The bubble burst in 2018 when a series of scandals involving an assistant basketball coach, the dean of the medical school, and the student Health Center's gynecologist led to the resignations of President Nikias and Provost Michael Quick. Some Institute board members worried about the effect these scandals would have on the Institute. It came to pass that there was no negative impact on the Institute. Donors seemed to understand that we were at, not of, USC. We continued to make progress in fundraising.

Despite being unable to go public with a capital campaign, we continued to build the Institute's board. We appointed Bro. Bernard J. Ploeger, SM, who was serving as the president of Chaminade University, the only Catholic university in all of Oceania except for two in Australia; John Bessolo, the president of his own accounting firm; and Scott Appleby, a historian who had just been appointed the Marilyn Keough Dean of the Keough School of Global Affairs at the University of Notre Dame. We also clarified how the standing committees of the board would function. Under the leadership of Ellen Hancock, the board approved mandates for each of its four standing committees. The Finance and Investment Committee put clearer protocols in place for tracking donations and investing the endowment. The addition of John Bessolo, a USC graduate and head of an accounting firm, brought greater sophistication to the board in these important areas. That same year, Fr. Martin Solma, SM, the Marianist provincial (my religious superior) and Dr. Dominic F. Doyle of the theology faculty of Boston College, added additional strengths to the board.

As a responsible board of directors, the issue of succession planning was kept on the agenda and discussed at almost every board meeting. The Governance and Nominating Committee drew up a list of six possible successors with the idea that one or two could be invited to become board members and prepared to assume the presidency of the Institute when needed. We also agreed upon a disaster plan that would sustain continuity of leadership should the president become incapacitated. The board often warned me to make sure that I kept in shape and took the three-week vacation time allowed in my contract. I rarely managed more than ten days of vacation.

One of the biggest surprises in the Catholic world was the resignation of Pope Benedict XVI and the election of Jorge Mario Bergoglio, the first pope from south of the equator, the first Jesuit ever elected, and the first to choose the name Francis. The election of Pope Francis brought something new to Church leadership—how new would soon become apparent, beginning with his free-style interaction with the public, his choice to live in an apartment rather than the papal palace, and his first encyclical, *Evangelii Gaudium*. He was a pastor rather than a theologian, someone close to the poor who cared about the environment and the fate of desperate migrants and refugees. At our fall board meeting, we had articles about Pope Francis and jumped into a lengthy and animated discussion about him. Some board members worried that his seeming anti-capitalism would negatively affect our fundraising efforts. Others were thrilled with his election and vision for the Church.

Coupled with this debate was the continuing problem of communicating the mission of the Institute in succinct ways accessible to the wider non-academic public. Some board members had trouble articulating the mission. One of the business leaders on the board thought that the very name of the Institute caused problems. He thought it would be much more inclusive to name ourselves the Institute for the Study of Religions. He believed that by saying we are Catholic we had put ourselves into a hole we would have to dig out of before we could persuade "open-minded" donors that our mission was not exclusive and narrow. Ultimately, we stuck with the title for several reasons. First, it was necessary to say where we were starting from. Where we start from is necessary to determine how we will and should proceed. Second, in the light of Vatican II, we needed to remember that the Catholic Church had affirmed religious freedom, called for ecumenism and interreligious dialogue, and endorsed lay leadership in the Church. Moreover, it is the largest non-governmental organization (NGO) in the world. We recalled the words of President Sample to the effect that among Christians, Catholics have the longest and richest intellectual tradition. Third, to speak of religion in general clarified little since we would then have to define religion (already an issue of debate), indicate which religion we were talking about, and then specify which school of interpretation within a particular religion (literalist, fundamentalist, liberal, prophetic). In short, including either *religion* or *Catholic* as part of the Institute's name presented its own difficulties.

The board continued to return to discussions about the mission and what it meant, not just to us but also to potential donors. At one point, the chair of the board believed that consulting a professional branding company would help. Though I expressed my doubts about whether this would help clarify our mission, another board member and I agreed to meet with experts in branding. We sent them some of our literature beforehand and then entered into a two-hour discussion with them. We tried to explain key aspects of the Catholic intellectual tradition, how it supports and contributes to interdisciplinary and interreligious dialogue, and why it enriches what most doctoral training leaves out—basic questions like the nature of the human person and the critical importance of theological and philosophical approaches to human wisdom. We even talked about major Catholic thinkers and the difference their lives and writings made for the Church. We were not communicating well with them. Our presentation drew blank stares.

They asked, "What's your elevator speech?" Creating a single sentence that adequately describes the unique mission of the Institute is not easy, especially for academics. Perhaps the problem was our own training as academics. We are used to writing articles and books, not articulating an intellectual tradition in one or two sentences. It is not that we did not make an effort to write three short sentences as an elevator speech followed by three additional short versions for three other audiences: the academy, the Church, and society (see appendix J). We agreed, however, to add a tag line to the name of the Institute: The Institute for Advanced Catholic Studies: Research, Dialogue, and Renewal.

A year after I stepped down from the presidency of the Institute, I tried once again to describe how an institution for Catholic research would understand its mission. In my book, *The Future of Catholic Higher Education: The Open Circle*,[2] I tried to give examples of what I consider to be the basic characteristics of the Catholic intellectual tradition. I was not making an elevator speech. Moreover, what I wrote was directed to faculty and administrators in Catholic colleges and universities.

I began by explaining that while many Catholics now have doctorates, few are Catholic intellectuals. It is also the case that members of other religions can understand well why the basic teachings of a religion could play an important and positive role in politics. Also, it is not just a matter of finding Catholic intellectuals. When I visit Catholic colleges and universities, I have often been asked, "What exactly is the Catholic intellectual tradition?" The word *exactly* makes the question impossible to answer. There

2. Heft, *Future*, 137.

is no one exact answer to that question. However, what I have tried to do in response is describe some of the assumptions made by thinkers influenced by the intellectual traditions of Catholicism.

What kind of assumptions? For example, they assume that theological and philosophical questions become more evident the more deeply scholars explore what it means to be human; that the more deeply they go into any area of scholarship, the more likely they will find it necessary to connect with other areas of knowledge. They also understand that the more intellectually vibrant religious traditions are, the more their followers learn. More specifically for Christian intellectuals, the doctrines of creation and the incarnation remain the theological focal points for all these assumptions. Catholic intellectuals, then, typically have a global sensibility, a sacramental imagination, an instinctive appreciation for both reason and faith, and a desire to integrate knowledge. Those who embrace the Catholic intellectual tradition find themselves in an ongoing conversation, often contentious, regularly multifaceted, and immensely diverse globally and culturally. They think less in terms of breaking news and clever sound bites, and more in terms of enduring truths wrestled from centuries of conversations with thinkers of other ages, as well as some from traditions other than Christianity.

To put all this in more theological and spiritual terms, scholars who probe the Catholic intellectual tradition ask common questions and affirm certain beliefs—for example, the transcendent character of the human person created in the image and likeness of God (which is also a fundamental teaching of Judaism and Islam). Catholic scholars study philosophies that are open to religious questions and theologies open to rational critique. For them, both faith and reason are important. Through the doctrine of creation, they recognize the sacramental character of all physical reality and therefore foster a nonmaterialistic but fully empirical approach to the sciences. Finally, Catholic intellectuals benefit from a sophisticated tradition of social ethics known in its modern form as Catholic social teaching. This body of teaching is necessarily universal and idealistic; therefore, it needs to be both contextualized and reframed to local political and economic realities. Consequently, it is neither imposed nor applied deductively. How to work for economic justice in Malawi will be different from how one works for it in Mongolia or Australia. Catholic social teaching is especially valuable for professional education and political and economic life. Again, while scholars do not need to be Catholic to appreciate, develop, and use these traditions, some committed Catholic intellectuals need to form an integral part of such an intellectual community. If there are no practicing Catholic intellectuals who help influence the tone and mission of the university, students will learn about a way of thinking but not witness a way of living, believing, and loving. As Pope Paul VI famously wrote in *Evangelii Nuntiandi*, "People listen to witnesses more than to teachers, but they listen most of all to teachers who are also witnesses."[3]

Since the time I tried to make clear to the branders what the mission of the Institute is, I have continued to think about another approach that might have been more effective, an approach that is not sufficiently included even in my own description of the Catholic intellectual tradition. Instead of relying on fundamental assumptions of that tradition which often are discussed in theological and philosophical ways—assumptions such as the compatibility of faith and reason and the centrality of the doctrines of creation and incarnation—there is another approach that needs to be added. It has more to do with practice than with doctrine. Two movements have contributed to this new emphasis: the rise of historical consciousness and the emphasis at Vatican II on the study of Scripture.

In the nineteenth century, Saint John Henry Newman (1801–1890) developed a fresh approach to the study of Catholicism in which he studied organically and historically. While studying the writings of the early thinkers in the Church, Newman became aware of the diversity between theological thinkers and the evolution of Christian teaching. In one of his few ecclesiological writings *The Lectures on the Prophetical Office of the Church* (1837) and

---

3. Paul VI, *Evangelii Nuntiandi*, para. 41.

even more in his revised preface to that book published in 1877, Newman built upon the traditional teaching of the three offices of Christ—namely, that through baptism all Christians are called to be priests, prophets, and kings. He affirmed a healthy tension among these three offices, a dynamism that can bear fruit when the inevitable tensions between them are balanced and interact in ways that mutually enrich the other.

Fifty years later, Friedrich von Hügel described religions as having institutional, intellectual, and mystical dimensions.[4] Both Newman and von Hügel believed that such dimensions needed to be kept in a dynamic balance, none cancelled out the other two or diminished what they contribute to the life of the Church. For example, when the office of the king dominates the others, or the office of the prophetic eclipses the sapiential, or a lack of the effective teaching of the faith contributes to superstition among the laity, the whole Church falls out of balance and becomes dysfunctional. Together, Newman and von Hügel opened up a positive role for dynamic tension as characteristic of a healthy Church or religion.[5]

More than any Church council, Vatican II articulated the need for *praxis* in general and social justice in particular, especially in *Gaudium et Spes*. It also emphasized a return to the study of Scripture—understood as a collection of writings that are mostly stories, history, psalms, and parables—not philosophical and theological concepts. Most importantly, for Christians, the New Testament was about a person, Jesus. It chronicles what he taught and what he did.

If one asks why Jesus died, two answers are typically given: He died to save us from our sins (a theological answer) or he died because of what he said and did (a prophetic answer). Both are true, but the prophetical reading makes us more aware that Jesus spoke truth to power, welcomed unseemly characters to table fellowship, and ignored religious restrictions regarding healing the sick, blind,

---

4. Hügel, "Three Elements of Religion."
5. Heft, "Tradition." Heft also cites Yves Congar and Avery Dulles who emphasize the importance of the prophetic dimension of the threefold office of Jesus.

and lame. The lives of the saints, narratives that illustrate doctrine, reflect the historical and prophetic living of faith.

The Catholic intellectual tradition is only now integrating a strong prophetic dimension into its self-understanding. The words and deeds of Jesus form the foundation for a fuller understanding of the Christian life rather than emphasizing only the intellectual dimensions. In its more recent form, this tradition, called Catholic social teaching, includes that emphasis on justice. Today, theologians worldwide emphasize the obligation of Christians to work for justice and be peacemakers.[6]

The value of the Catholic intellectual tradition, therefore, is not only a matter of understanding, of Logos. It is also a matter of witness and deeds of justice, of *praxis*. In his teachings and deeds, Pope Francis has made this especially clear. He has shocked many Catholics by declaring that no war is just, that all wars are destructive. The difficulty of integrating a typical presentation of the Catholic intellectual tradition (e.g., the Just War Theory) and Catholic social teaching (justice and peacemaking) is evident in the US Bishops 1983 pastoral *The Challenge of Peace*, where these two emphases were treated separately—but not integrated.[7] The Catholic intellectual tradition must be, therefore, more than intellectual. Perhaps the dynamic relationship between priest, prophet, and king and a deeper integration of intellectual and biblical traditions will constitute a more adequate representation of how Catholics should think and act.

I am not so naïve as to think that if I had articulated the mission of the Institute in this more historical and prophetic way that the branders would have understood the mission of the Institute and produced a catchy elevator speech. What has become clearer, however, is that donors give to credible people, with or without an elevator speech, to people who are passionate about and committed to an important mission. Fundraising is more about friendship than elevator speeches.

---

6. Prusak and Reed-Bouley, *Catholic Higher Education*.
7. National Conference of Catholic Bishops, *The Challenge of Peace*.

The success of the Institute, however that might be best described, depended greatly on the friendships we were able to develop, not just with donors but also with the leadership of USC. One very important friendship was that with President Steven Sample, who welcomed us to USC. As he stepped down as president in 2010, the university appropriately celebrated his great achievements, providing him with an office on campus, and made it possible for his longtime assistant to continue to help him.

Though not Catholic, he was a serious Christian. Around the time he became president of USC, he had become a member of the Episcopalian Church where he was invited on two occasions to give a sermon. He gave an extraordinary commencement address the year that he retired. He told the graduates that he wanted to talk about their personal development as human beings because a "person's ultimate success is not so much about his professional abilities or political brilliance as it is his character." He then proceeded to ask the students three questions: how do you feel about money? How do you feel about children, both those you will someday call your own and those of your neighbors as well? And finally, how do you feel about God? Having raised the third question, he said, "Say what? God? Did he say God? Why would anyone bring up God at a secular commencement ceremony?" He responded to his question by saying that he worried that too many people simply duck the question.

I made it a point after he retired to have lunch with him in his office every month. Given the seriousness with which he took matters of religion and faith, I should not have been surprised that Catholicism became a regular part of our conversations. He asked many questions about conscience, dogmas, hierarchy, moral teachings, confession, and the Eucharist. I answered his questions as best I could.

During the second semester of my first year at USC, I taught a course on the history of the issues that Catholic immigrants had to deal with in coming to the United States in the nineteenth century. Sample's wife, Kathryn, and one of his daughters, Elizabeth, audited the class; both had converted to Catholicism several years before. Thank God I did not have to give them grades for auditing. I can only imagine some of the conversations at their dinner table.

One day, after many of these lunch conversations, he said, "I'm ready." I asked, "Ready for what?" He replied, "I'm ready to become a Catholic." He smiled broadly and I had tears in my eyes. I wasn't trying to convert him; all I did was answer his many questions as best I could.

Several weeks later, we organized a simple service based on the affirmation of the Apostles Creed. His wife, one of his daughters, his assistant, and some Carmelite sisters attended the ceremony. By then, he had to use a wheelchair to get around. I was waiting for him as he wheeled up the aisle. As I welcomed him, he said in a loud voice, "You won!" I replied, "Neither of us has won. We are both graced."

Diagnosed with Parkinson's in the fall of 2001, President Sample died on March 29, 2016. The funeral celebration was held in the Los Angeles Cathedral on April 8. Over two thousand people attended. I preached. In retrospect, had not major USC figures such as Joseph Aoun, Cornelius (Neal) Pings, Kevin Starr, Stanley Gold, and Marianist high school graduate and later Institute board member Tom Condon worked with Sample to invite us to locate the Institute at USC, I doubt it would have survived. He supported it in many ways, all the time recognizing its independence.

Sample's successor, Max Nikias, was and has remained a great advocate for the Institute as was Beth Garrett as provost, Alan Kreditor, the vice president for advancement, and most recently, Amber Miller, the dean of the Dornsife College of Letters, Arts, and Sciences. The irony that a non-Catholic university strongly supported the Institute for Advanced Catholic Studies should not be lost. I will always be grateful for their support, mentorship, and friendship.

# 11

# On a Roll
## —People and Programs (2015–2020)

WITH THE ASSOCIATE DIRECTOR of research Gary Adler's departure for Penn State in 2015, it became evident that we needed someone who could oversee running the office and its finances, and to help organize programs and the annual lecture series. We constructed the job description and hired a national search firm to generate top candidates. In May of 2018, after interviewing four finalists, we hired Dr. Becky Cerling, a medieval historian, Presbyterian minister, and a Benedictine Oblate, as our executive director. She was ecumenical by nature. She met important needs of the Institute: good organizational skills and careful financial oversight. She also freed me to focus more of my time raising money for operating expenses and building the endowment.

Early in 2014, we began discussions about organizing a prototype of what we hoped the Institute might look like when it would have scholars in residence. We invited three scholars, a Muslim, a Catholic, and a Jew, to spend a fall semester at USC doing research together, learning from each other, giving presentations, visiting classes together, and talking with students (see appendix K).

Amir Hussain, Wilhelmus (Pim) Valkenburg, and Rabbi Reuven Firestone

During the spring of 2015, they frequently met by Zoom and also twice in person to discuss what kinds of outreach they would create with USC and the broader Los Angeles communities. We invited the Catholic Campus Ministry community of USC, now named the Caruso Catholic Center (CCC), to join us in this effort, share the cost, and provide office space for the scholars. They graciously agreed.

The scholars had to arrange semester sabbaticals with each of their universities so that they could spend that time together at USC. Two were from Los Angeles and the third from the East Coast. Over the next eight months, they worked together to create programs for the fall 2016 semester. The CCC set aside space for work places on the second floor of its new building. Buying the time of three scholars for a semester was expensive, a total cost of $250,000. Everyone who worked with them or attended the many events that they organized gave them rave reviews. We never used endowment money to support this program.

We found that few of the Catholic students involved in USC campus ministry showed much interest in these programs. The programming of Campus Ministry did not emphasize the importance of an intellectual understanding of the faith. Nor were there any programs devoted to issues of interreligious dialogue, social justice, racism, or sexism. The campus ministers were very capable and dedicated, but like so many campus ministry programs (and I include those at Catholic universities), there was little effort to develop the intellectual understanding of the life of faith. At the same time, it is often hard to find faculty who are excellent in their disciplines and also raise serious questions about morality and religion. The faculty at USC were, however, responsive and attended many of the sessions, along with the wider public.

For the Institute, certainly, the issue of passing on the faith in various religious traditions remained an important area of research. In early 2016, Dr. Jan Stets, a sociological social psychologist at the University of California, Riverside, and I organized an interdisciplinary study of the rapidly growing number of young adults who were no longer affiliated with any religious tradition, later published as *Empty Churches: Non-Affiliation in America*. We had established a profile of the scholars that we invited to become a part of our interdisciplinary research programs. First of all, we invited scholars who in their particular disciplines were recognized for the high quality of their research. Second, we made sure that we had both men and women in the group. Third, we worked at also including young and old scholars. In this important research project, for example, ten men and nine women contributed chapters. They represented various academic disciplines: communications, history, mathematics, social and developmental psychology, philosophy and theology, sociology, gerontology, and "parenting" (two Catholic women who were trying to raise their sons and daughters in the faith fully participated in all the discussions of the scholars and contributed their own chapters).

In 2017, we learned that Pope Francis would devote the next international synod of bishops held in 2018 to the Church's relationship to young people in the Church. Archbishop Gomez of Los Angeles was selected as one of the bishops to attend the synod. We were able to put together a pamphlet that highlighted the conclusions of our research and sent to Rome enough copies for all the synod participants (see appendix L).

In 2018, the Institute launched another "True Wealth of Nations" research project on the meaning of justice. Dan Finn, board member and the leader of the project, thought that justice needed to be rethought for democratic, secular, and religiously pluralistic societies. The traditional Catholic teaching on justice drew mainly from Thomas Aquinas (1225–1274), who lived in a feudal society. At that time, Christianity in the West (Europe) was more or less unified. In Christendom, the king was expected to be accountable to the pope for the just treatment of the citizens. The formation of nation states and the Enlightenment created a very different social and political context for the life of not just a European Church, but for an ever-expanding global Church.

Dan Finn invited scholars from Africa, India, South America, Europe, and the United States to explore the meaning of justice in a secular, pluralistic, globalized culture. Most of our interdisciplinary research projects required that the scholars meet with one another in person for one day to talk about how, from their particular discipline, they would address the issue. Eight months later, drafts of the papers were due, bound together and distributed to all to read before they met a second time for four days. They were usually given two to three months to read all the drafts and prepare for discussions. COVID made it nearly impossible to meet in person, so these meetings had to be postponed. Only in 2023 were the scholars able to reassemble and spend several days together discussing their papers with each other. That important research has been published as *Rethinking Justice in Catholic Social Thought*.

In 2019 we launched the fourth GID program, which the executive director organized and led. The senior scholar was the Jesuit Fr. John Coleman, an expert in the sociology of religion.

We publicized how, through this and previous GID programs, a sustained interaction between a senior scholar and a small group of young scholars proved helpful to them in shaping their professional and spiritual lives.

For twenty years, we had kept an eye out for sites for a possible residential center for the Institute. Before making the decision to locate the Institute at USC, we had already looked at properties in Princeton and Washington, DC. In Los Angeles, while living with the Vincentians from 2006–2012, I often walked by an impressive Tudor-style stone building owned by USC named the Kerkoff Mansion. It was only half occupied. Next door to it was an apartment building also owned by USC. We talked with USC about renting the other half only to discover that the donors, the Kerkoff Family, had restricted the use of the building to the university's communications faculty.

In 2019, we looked seriously at a second property, a 1.7-acre site located just five blocks from the USC campus. There were several buildings on the property: an old mansion on the record of historical buildings, an empty primary school, and a three-story residence hall for students. The Sisters of the Company of Mary owned the property and wanted to sell.

We asked two donors who were good friends of the Institute, Ed Roski and Jack Baker, both experts in commercial real estate transactions, to enter into conversation with us and the Sisters about buying the property. The Sisters listed the entire property and buildings at $17 million. That price was much more than we could afford, so we offered them $8 million for a part of the property which housed the mansion, the grade school (which we would raze), and some land. They did not accept our offer. They wanted to sell the entire property with all its buildings. We know that subsequently they sold the property to a developer who specializes in building student housing.

In 2019, USC, trying to recover from the scandals, appointed a new president and provost. I reported directly to the dean of the USC Dornsife College of Letters, Arts, and Sciences, Dr. Amber D. Miller, who had assumed that position in July 2016, and proved to be a great friend to the Institute. Despite the turnover of presidents at USC, the support of the university for the Institute has remained constant.

# 12

# Stepping Down as President

IN 1977, AT THE University of Toronto, I finished my dissertation on the historical origins of the doctrine of papal infallibility, a study of the first third of the fourteenth century when the papacy was located in Avignon, France. I immediately began teaching at the University of Dayton where I would spend the next twenty-nine years of my life.

Around 1980, I received a call from the president of the University of Dayton, Bro. Raymond L. Fitz, SM. He asked me if I would serve on a university-wide task force that was to rethink the Catholic and Marianist nature and mission of the university. I agreed. Then he asked if I would be willing to chair the task force. I agreed. Little did I realize then that I would spend the better part of my life thinking about the nature and mission of Catholic universities.

Nor would I have guessed what would begin to unfold in the coming years. A new adventure and formidable challenge began in 1995 when representatives of a major foundation contacted me to talk about the best ways to strengthen the mission of Catholic higher education—conversations that led me to leave the University of Dayton in 2006 to establish and build the Institute for

Advanced Catholic Studies at USC, where I remained for the next seventeen years.

At the Institute's spring board meeting in 2018, I told the board that it was time to find a new president. I was in good health and still had the necessary energy to continue, but I realized that it was time. Knowing that replacing the founder of a successful start-up operation has frequently proven difficult, I thought suggesting a two-year lead time would guarantee enough time for the board to do a good job in finding the next president of the Institute.

In my report to the board in October 2019, I explained in more detail why I thought that it was a good time for me to retire. I told them that our staff and the board were stronger than ever, and that we had been modestly successful in building the endowment. During the previous five years, we had received additional pledges for fellowships, so that by 2020, the endowment was approaching $10 million. Big gifts take a long time, and for the Institute, a $1.5 million gift (the amount needed for a fellowship) was the biggest that we had received. The Institute has remained committed to building the endowment and will continue to look at possible sites for a residential center where we can welcome scholars to spend an academic year with other scholars doing research and deepening their appreciation of Catholicism as a rich intellectual and spiritual tradition.

In 1939, Abraham Flexner, the first president of the Institute for Advanced Study at Princeton, made a case for scholars having the time and the freedom to create useless knowledge. In recent years, instead of speaking of useless knowledge, we speak of "basic research." In today's Catholic universities, we distinguish between liberal and professional education. The research fostered by the Institute is and will always be both liberal and practical. While the Christian tradition supports contemplation, Jesus's great commandment is love—a typical example of the Catholic both/and principle.

I have spent all my adult life exploring, explaining, and trying to strengthen the Catholic intellectual tradition as best I can. It is especially a privilege to build an institution whose only purpose is to strengthen the Catholic intellectual tradition in Catholic colleges and universities for the sake of the universal Church and society. The Institute for Advanced Catholic Studies exists to support that effort on every Catholic campus and offer it to the wider academic community—communities like USC, a private, nonreligiously affiliated university whose non-Catholic leadership saw the value of the Institute for their own university, for the Catholic and other religious traditions, and for global conversations.

As I explained at the end of chapter 4, I was not pleased with the report that a Jesuit wrote for the foundation comparing several institutes dedicated to strengthening Catholic intellectual life in the United States. In retrospect, I have come to think that what he wrote at the end of his report about the Institute has turned out to be true:

> Over time it may grow into a mature research institute as envisioned by its founders, but it should not be judged a failure if it does not achieve them in the short and medium term since a quick review of other institutes for advanced studies will show that they at their origin trod much the same gradual path to excellence.

# Appendices

A   Prospectus: Institute for Advanced Catholic Studies
B   Commission on Catholic Scholarship
C   Board of Trustees and Academic Advisory Council
D   The Need and The Benefits
E   John T. Noonan Jr. *America* Article
F   Correspondence with Archbishop Pilarczyk Re: Cardinal Ratzinger
G   IACS Book Offerings
H   Generations in Dialogue Program
I    Endowed Fellowships
J   Elevator Speech
K   World Religions: Finding Common Ground Program
L   Youth, the Catholic Church, and Our Future
M  2017 IACS Board of Trustees
N   2023 IACS Board of Trustees

The full appendices are available in color at: https://dornsife.usc.edu/iacs/IACShistory.

# Appendix A
## Prospectus: Institute for Advanced Catholic Studies

Full document available in color at:
https://dornsife.usc.edu/iacs/IACShistory

THE
INSTITUTE
FOR ADVANCED
CATHOLIC
STUDIES

PROSPECTUS

### Origins

The proposal to establish in the United States of America an Institute for Advanced Catholic Studies is, to use the phrasing suggested by the Code of Canon Law, an "initiative of the faithful" intended for the common good of the Church in its performance of the increasingly significant roles it is called upon to play as a participant in the development of modern cultures around the globe. The idea for the Institute was inspired by the Church's embrace of both the problems and the possibilities of contemporary life. It is grounded in the sense of responsibility that issued refreshed from the Second Vatican Council's reaffirmation of the sacred dignity not only of the Catholic faithful, but of all human persons in all traditions in all societies throughout the world. Finally, as an institutional design of a specialized and particular kind, it is a response to the call for a renewal of Christian intellectual life voiced in *Ex Corde Ecclesiae*, specifically its encouragement to devise the new forms of institutional capacity required for the ongoing task of "cooperation between Catholic universities and other universities, and with other research and educational institutions, both private and governmental."

The Institute's aim is to contribute to the fulfillment of this need for cooperation in the vital sector of scholarly research on all aspects of Catholic life and thought, past and present. That purpose is premised on the confident hope that in its continuing encounter with the pluralism of modern life, the voice of the Catholic Church in public dialogue will be enhanced by the fruits that come from the hard work of scholarship and critical reflection rooted within the Catholic tradition. The watchword *aggiornamento* brings with it a new duty on the part of the Church to

# Appendix B
## Commission on Catholic Scholarship
Also available at: https://dornsife.usc.edu/iacs/IACShistory

## COMMISSION ON CATHOLIC SCHOLARSHIP

The members of the Commission on Catholic Scholarship accepted the challenge of developing the concept of an Institute for Advanced Catholic Studies and exploring the feasibility of its establishment. Over a period of two years, working in five subcommittees, they produced this Prospectus as their final report.

### MEMBERS

JAMES L. HEFT, SM — CHAIR
*University Chair in Faith and Culture and Chancellor, University of Dayton; Chair, Board of Directors of the Association of Catholic Colleges and Universities*

MICHAEL J. LACEY — VICE-CHAIR
*Director of United States Studies, Woodrow Wilson Center, Washington, DC*

GEORGIA M. KEIGHTLEY — EXECUTIVE DIRECTOR
*Associate Professor of Theology, Trinity College, Washington, DC*

R. SCOTT APPLEBY
*Associate Professor of History; Director of the Cushwa Center for the Study of American Catholicism, University of Notre Dame; Fellow of the Joan B. Kroc Institute for International Peace Studies, University of Notre Dame*

ANTHONY BRENNINKMEYER
*Humanitas Foundation, New York, New York*

WILLIAM J. BYRON, SJ
*Former President of the Catholic University of America, now Distinguished Professor of Management, Georgetown University; Founding Director and Past Chair, Bread for the World*

MICHAEL J. BUCKLEY, SJ
*Canisius Professor of Systematic Theology and Director of the Jesuit Institute, Boston College; Past President, Catholic Theological Society of America; Life Member, Clare Hall, Cambridge University*

LISA SOWLE CAHILL
*J. Donald Monan, SJ, Professor at Boston College; Fellow, American Academy of Arts and Sciences; Past President, Society of Christian Ethics, Catholic Theological Society of America*

PAUL CARON
*Executive Director, CEMA; Chairman, Unisun*

JOHN COLEMAN, SJ
*Charles Casassa Chair in Social Values, Loyola-Marymount University, Los Angeles; Former Chair in American Culture and Values, University of Louvain, Belgium and holder, Bannon Chair, University of Santa Clara*

JAMES CONNOR, SJ
*Director, Woodstock Theological Center, Georgetown University*

ALICE GALLIN, OSU
*Visiting Research Scholar, The Catholic University of America; Former Executive Director, Association of Catholic Colleges and Universities*

PHILIP GLEASON
*Professor emeritus of History, University of Notre Dame; Past President, American Catholic Historical Association; President, Immigration and Ethnic History Society*

DORIS GOTTEMOELLER, RSM
*Former President of the Sisters of Mercy of the Americas; Chairperson Catholic Health Association; Member, International Policy Committee, United States Catholic Conference; Past President, Leadership Conference of Women Religious*

NATHAN O. HATCH
*Provost, University of Notre Dame; Charles Warren Fellow, Harvard University*

REV. J. BRYAN HEHIR
*Professor of the Practice in Religion and Society, Harvard University Center for International Affairs and Harvard Divinity School; Fellow, American Academy of Arts and Sciences*

MONIKA HELLWIG
*Executive Director, Association of Catholic Colleges and Universities; Professor of Theology Emerita, Georgetown University; Past President, Catholic Theological Society of America; Former Fellow, Woodrow Wilson International Center for Scholars*

DERMOT KEOGH
*Professor of History, University College, Cork, Ireland; Former Fellow, Woodrow Wilson International Center for Scholars*

REV. JOSEPH A. KOMONCHAK
*John C. and Gertrude P. Hubbard Professor of Theology, Department of Religion and Religious Education, The Catholic University of America; Former Fellow, Woodrow Wilson International Center for Scholars*

JOHN T. NOONAN
*Judge of the United States Court of Appeals for the Ninth Circuit and Robbins Professor of Law, Emeritus, University of California, Berkeley; Fellow, American Academy of Arts and Sciences; President, Thomas More-Jacques Maritain Institutes; Former President, American Catholic Philosophical Association*

FRANCIS OAKLEY
*Edward Dorr Griffin Professor of the History of Ideas and President Emeritus, Williams College; Fellow of the Medieval Academy of America and former Chair of the American Council of Learned Societies; Fellow, American Academy of Arts and Sciences*

DAVID J. O'BRIEN
*Professor of History and Loyola Professor of Roman Catholic Studies, College of the Holy Cross; Past President, American Catholic Historical Association; Member, National Conference of Catholic Bishops Task Force on Catholic Education and Catholic Social Teaching*

TIMOTHY O'MEARA
*Howard J. Kenna, CSC, Professor of Mathematics and Provost Emeritus, University of Notre Dame; Fellow, American Academy of Arts and Sciences*

KATARINA SCHUTH, OSF
*Endowed Chair for the Social Scientific Study of Religion, St. Paul Seminary School of Divinity, University of St. Thomas; Member, Executive Committee, Association of Theological Schools*

WILLIAM M. SHEA
*Professor and former Chair, Department of Theology, St. Louis University; Past President, College Theology Society; Former Fellow, Woodrow Wilson International Center for Scholars*

MARGARET O'BRIEN STEINFELS
*Editor of Commonweal*

CHARLES TAYLOR
*Professor Emeritus of Philosophy, McGill University; Foreign Honorary Member, American Academy of Arts and Sciences; 1999 Gifford Lecturer*

DAVID TRACY
*Andrew Thomas Greeley and Grace McNichols Greeley Distinguished Service Professor of Roman Catholic Studies and Professor of Theology; Professor in the Committee on the Analysis of Ideas and Methods and in the Committee on Social Thought, University of Chicago; Fellow, American Academy of Arts and Sciences*

# Appendix C
## Board of Trustees and Academic Advisory Council

Also available at: https://dornsife.usc.edu/iacs/IACShistory

### BOARD OF TRUSTEES ACADEMIC ADVISORY COUNCIL

#### BOARD OF TRUSTEES

Paul Caron, Treasurer
*Executive Director, CEMA*

Hugh Dempsey, K.M., Assistant Treasurer
*Vice President for Institutional Advancement, IACS*

James H. Duffy, Secretary
*Retired Attorney/Finance & Banking; Writer*

James L. Heft, S.M., Chair
*President & Founding Director, IACS*

Michael J. Lacey
*Senior Scholar, Woodrow Wilson Center*

John T. Noonan, First Vice-Chair
*Judge of the US Court of Appeals, Ninth Circuit*

Francis Oakley, Vice-Chair
*President Emeritus, Williams College*

Arogyaswami Paulraj
*Chairman/CTO, Iospan Wireless; Professor, Stanford University*

Kevin Starr
*University Professor, University of Southern California; California State Librarian*

#### ACADEMIC ADVISORY COUNCIL

Mary Douglas
*Anthropologist, London, England*

Dagfinn Follesdal
*Stanford University, Clarence Irving Lewis Professor of Philosophy*

Roberto Goizueta
*Professor, Boston College, Department of Theology*

Patrick A. Heelan, S.J.
*Georgetown University, William Gaston Professor of Philosophy*

M. Cathleen Kaveny
*John P. Murphy Foundation Professor of Law & Professor of Theology, University of Notre Dame*

Reverend Joseph Komonchak
*The Catholic University of America Department of Religion and Religious Education*

Most Reverend Oscar H. Lipscomb
*Archbishop, Mobile, Alabama*

Bernard McGinn
*Professor, University of Chicago, Divinity School*

Michael Novak
*American Enterprise Institute George Frederick Jewett Scholar in Religion, Philosophy & Public Policy*

Most Reverend Daniel E. Pilarczyk
*Archbishop, Cincinnati, Ohio*

Ernesto Rossi
*European Businessman*

Kevin Starr
*University Professor, University of Southern California; California State Librarian*

Charles Taylor
*Professor, McGill University, Department of Philosophy*

David Tracy
*Professor, University of Chicago, Divinity School*

# Appendix D
## The Need and The Benefits

Full document available in color at:
https://dornsife.usc.edu/iacs/IACShistory

# Appendix E

## John T. Noonan Jr. *America* Article

Full document available at:
https://dornsife.usc.edu/iacs/IACShistory

Here faith and reason could hand in hand explore the implications of Catholicism.

# An Institute for Advanced Catholic Studies

— BY JOHN T. NOONAN JR. —

FAITH AND REASON ARE COMPANIONS indispensable to each other on Catholicism's journey from Jerusalem. To understand the implications of faith, to relate the constructions of reason to these implications, the two must go hand in hand. One kind of institutional setting in which such understanding and relationships could fruitfully be explored is an institute for advanced studies.

I want to do three things here: first, to argue the advantages of such an institute by analogy with existing independent institutes, sketching their special characteristics; second, to show the particular good of an institute for advanced Catholic studies; and, finally, to offer the comfort of examples from the past of comparable Catholic educational enterprises.

JOHN T. NOONAN JR. *is a is a member of the Commission on Catholic Scholarship.*

# Appendix F
## Correspondence with Archbishop Pilarczyk Re: Cardinal Ratzinger

THE INSTITUTE FOR ADVANCED CATHOLIC STUDIES

April 2, 2001

Archbishop Daniel Pilarczyk
Archdiocese of Cincinnati

Fax: 513-421-7537

Dear Dan,

Attached is a copy of what I would send to the CDF concerning the Institute for Advanced Catholic Studies. I have little understanding of what should be sent. I am counting on your experience with these sorts of things (I trust that it is not that extensive) to provide the editing needed to make the most effective response. I have numbered the paragraphs. The last one, about me, might not be appropriate to include–but again, I don't know about these things.

I have also FAXed to you a copy of a letter that Fr. Joe Komonchak of Catholic University wrote to the editors of the National Catholic Register, a newspaper owned then and now by the Legionnaires of Christ. At first, they refused to publish it; I called the editor and told him that if they did not publish it in its entirety in their very next issue, I would have a copy of the letter on every US bishop's desk within 24 hours. He finally relented, but then, in that next issue, added his own commentary to try to blunt the effect of having so many of their distortions and outright errors about the Institute exposed by Komonchak's letter. This letter will give you a better idea of the kind of irresponsible criticism we got from the right (the NCR has been relatively quiet since then). I also believe that the folks who have contributed to these articles (including Fr. Matthew Lamb of Boston College, a confidant of Cardinal Law) are likely to be the same ones who more recently have brought their complaints directly to the CDF.

On another matter, the board of the IACS met this last Friday in DC. Among the issues we discussed was the presentation we are to make on the 16th of May to the Board of Argidius in Amsterdam. While they all appreciate immensely your thoughtful support of the Institute, they and I do not think it necessary that you fly to Holland for the meeting. We think that a 3-5 minute video from you would be both sufficient and very helpful. I want to wait a little longer before I make any suggestions to you as to what you might say in the video. In another week or so, I will be hearing from a member of the family who will be talking with some members of the Board; I will learn from him some of the points that might most fruitfully be pressed by you and will get in touch with you then.

I have submitted my article on our meeting here with you to the other NCR, the National Catholic Reporter, but haven't heard anything from them yet.

In the meantime, let us continue to work together for the sake of the kingdom.

Sincerely,

Jim

James L. Heft, S.M.
Chairman: Institute for Advanced Catholic Studies

Office of the Chairman
University of Dayton • 300 College Park • Dayton, OH 45469-1549
Phone 937.229.2105 • Fax 937.229.4906 • Email heft@udayton.edu

**Draft of Response Written by James Heft, S.M., for
Archbishop Daniel Pilarczyk to CDF's Inquiry about
the Institute for Advanced Catholic Studies**

(1) I believe that the proposed Institute for Advanced Catholic Studies will be of great benefit to the Church and the Catholic colleges and universities in the United States, as well as in other parts of the world. Those who are leading this effort have identified a great need in the Church today: the development of a deeper understanding of the wisdom of the Catholic intellectual tradition among Catholic scholars from a variety of academic disciplines. They plan to work not only at the intellectual level; they will also include an on-going spiritual formation for scholars as well. For too long, scholars have suffered a type of schizophrenia between their intellectual work and their spiritual life. The Institute will be a place where the intellectual dimension will be rooted in Catholicism's deep and broad traditions, and the spiritual dimension will be celebrated through the ministrations of a full-time chaplain who understands both the intellectual and the spiritual life, and their integral relationship. The Institute, therefore, will have not only a library, but also a chapel; not only scholars, but also a chaplain.

(2) The attached Prospectus explains why this Institute is needed. We are all painfully aware that in North America and Europe the number of priests and religious is rapidly declining. In the United States, most of its over 200 Catholic colleges and universities were founded by religious communities. Now, few of those communities are numerous enough to lead much less staff these institutions. Lay persons are increasingly teaching and leading these institutions, but in many instances are doing so with only a superficial understanding of Catholicism and what the mission of a Catholic university should be. The leading Catholic universities in the United States run the greatest risk of becoming secular, while the majority of the rest, many of them quite small and with limited resources, run the risk either of going out of business or of requiring teachers to do so much teaching that serious scholarship is nearly impossible. In the cases of both, the leading and the struggling universities, serious development of Catholic intellectual life is to a large extent missing. There is a great need, therefore, for a different kind of institution, a research institute, whose sole purpose is to provide scholars with the time and financial support to develop a deeper sense of what the Catholic intellectual tradition can offer to their lives as professors at Catholic colleges and universities.

(3) Besides scholars in Catholic colleges and universities, another group of scholars will, I believe, benefit a great deal from the proposed Institute: those who teach in secular universities. It is unfortunate that some of the most respected Catholic scholars have chosen, for a variety of reasons, not to teach in Catholic universities. They too need to be brought together with other scholars committed to studying the Catholic intellectual tradition so that they might be able to bring into open conversation both their intellectual work and their spiritual life– precisely something they are unable to do at their secular campuses. I believe that such an integrated experience will lead at least some of them to join faculties at Catholic colleges and universities.

(4) Finally, it is important to realize what this Institute is not. It is neither a college nor a university. It will not have any students, nor will it teach any courses. It is neither a theological

nor a philosophical institute. It will not, as an Institute for advanced Catholic studies, take positions itself on matters in the Church or on theological questions. Its purpose, rather, is to provide twenty to twenty-five scholars from different disciplines an opportunity to focus for a full academic year on their research as it relates to the Catholic tradition. The aim is that these scholars will then return to their respective institutions renewed and filled with a deeper understanding of what Catholicism means for their discipline, for the Church and for modern society. They will also have formed an intellectual community that strengthens them in their conviction that Catholicism offers a distinctive and rich vision of the intellectual life.

(5) I realize that the Institute has received some criticism. I believe, however, that such criticism has been misplaced. Part of the confusion is due to a coincidence. Just when the Institute went public two years ago with its effort to raise money for its endowment, the media, both secular and Catholic, depicted in a highly polarized fashion the discussions of the final stages of the implementation of Ex corde ecclesiae. As a consequence of this coincidence in timing, the Institute appeared to some like a reaction against the implementation of Ex corde when in fact the planning for it had begun long before.

(6) Some people also apparently believe that the Institute will become, in its desire to be "independent", a very sophisticated platform for dissident theologians. Early in 1997, it formed a Commission on Catholic Scholarship composed of 25 Catholic scholars and leaders in Catholic higher education. The Commission's task was to develop the concept of the Institute; the completion of its task was the writing of the Prospectus. One or two members of that Commission, dissolved since late 1998, were described by reporters of the National Catholic Register to be dissident theologians.

(7) Nevertheless, the Institute does want to be independent--not from the guidance and influence of the Church, but rather from the internecine competition that too frequently characterizes US Catholic colleges and universities. Standing apart from Catholic college and universities, the Institute can have its greatest impact upon them. To insure that their independence nevertheless remains sensitive to the needs of the Church, I and another archbishop have been invited to be members of its Academic Advisory Board, and once it begins to expand its own governing Board, bishops will be invited to be members of it as well.

(8) Concerning the Institute's impact on Catholic theology, I think it should be quite positive. It is likely that among the 20 to 25 scholars who come each year, several will be theologians. Scholarship will be done at the highest level. My experience tells me that most of our trouble with theologians arises when they become captive of various movements and trends, be they feminist or liberationist or restorationist. Being in sustained conversation with excellent scholars in other disciplines will broaden theologians' horizons and provide especially fertile ground for the dialogue between faith and culture. Second, it will also require theologians to work at a high level of excellence, and at a more faithful and creative appropriation of the tradition. Third and finally, it should help us to bridge some of the ideological divides that exist among theologians, especially in the United States.

9) Finally, I have known for nearly twenty-five years Fr. James Heft, S.M., who is

leading this effort. He is an orthodox Catholic theologian who has done much in my archdiocese and throughout the United States to provide sane and prudent guidance to many students and teachers on a wide range of issues. In the first published review of his doctoral thesis on the historical origins of papal infallibility, the late Yves Congar wrote that his understanding of infallibility was "exact." Recently, Fr. Heft wrote an article encouraging Catholic theologians in the United States to accept the mandatum. He is also a leader in Catholic higher education, having served recently as the chair of the Board of Directors of the Association of Catholic Colleges and Universities. His leadership is still another reason why I am confident that the Institute will be a great asset for the Church and Catholic higher education, not only in this country, but elsewhere in the world as well.

April 1, 2001
Archbishop Daniel Pilarczyk

# Appendix G
## IACS Book Offerings

Full document available in color at:
https://dornsife.usc.edu/iacs/IACShistory

# Appendix H
## Generations in Dialogue Program

Full document available in color at:
https://dornsife.usc.edu/iacs/IACShistory

## Creating Mullin Scholars

### Summer 2013

Generations in Dialogue and the Impact of Mentoring on Academics and Artists Who Care About Faith

In the fall of 2010, with the generous support of Peter Mullin, the Institute for Advanced Catholic Studies launched the **Generations in Dialogue** program with a purpose that was both simple and profound: to create a multi-generational community that would allow participants – following the example set by the traditions of the Catholic Church – to explore how faith informs scholarship and scholarship informs faith. Today, this rich, intergenerational experiment is in its third year and going stronger than ever, thanks in no small part to Mullin's personal commitment to mentoring and forming leaders, which has served as the program's inspiration.

Through GID, young, early-career scholars are given the opportunity to meet and speak with, listen to and learn from some of the finest and most experienced minds in their fields. In turn, these mentors have the opportunity to pass on their accumulated wisdom and experience to a generation of scholars at the dawn of their professions—artists and educators who are eager to learn how to integrate their faith into their academic, artistic and intellectual lives.

Over the course of two years and four weekend-long sessions, these young scholars engage in intensive and intimate dialogue with their peers and mentors, who guide them through scholarly discussions, personal reflection, professional advisement, and shared prayer. Through these encounters, participants have an opportunity to cultivate a creative scholarship that engages the intellectual and spiritual traditions of Catholicism, as well as foster a lifelong commitment to serving others—tools that enable them to turn a profession into a vocation.

Upon completing the program, the participants become "Mullin Scholars" at the Institute and are invited to engage in future Institute research and writing projects. They are invited to stay in contact with their mentor and become a part of a larger community of scholars.

# Appendix I
## Endowed Fellowships

Full document available in color at:
https://dornsife.usc.edu/iacs/IACShistory

An overview of

Endowed Fellowships at the

**Institute for Advanced Catholic Studies**

at The University of Southern California

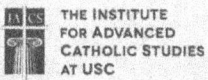

THE INSTITUTE
FOR ADVANCED
CATHOLIC STUDIES
AT USC

# Appendix J
## Elevator Speech

### The Institute for Advanced Catholic Studies

### What is its Purpose?

1. "Elevator Speech":
    a. There are lots of intellectuals with little or no interest in religion.
    b. There are lots of religious people with not interest in the intellectual life.
    c. The Institute seeks to form more intellectuals with a deep interest in religion.

2. For the Academy:
    a. Provide support, financial and professional, for scholars interested in the study of religion, especially Catholicism.
    b. Provide support for the study of theology and philosophy and the history of religion as a normal part of academic life.
    c. Provide support for the careful study of the sciences, especially biological and neurological, especially as they relate to ethical and theological traditions.

3. For the Church:
    a. Provide intellectual leadership rooted in the Catholic Tradition
    b. Provide structured and thoughtful dialogue with other Christians and other religions.
    c. Provide a community of scholars capable of a sustained and dedicated dialogue between faith and culture.

4. For Society:
    a. Provide a sustained and thoughtful exploration of ethical and religious perspectives that will contribute to a deeper understanding of the common good.
    b. Provide an international center where perspectives of justice and human rights rooted in the Catholic tradition will engage economic and political issues.

# Appendix K
## World Religions: Finding Common Ground Program

Full document available in color at:
https://dornsife.usc.edu/iacs/IACShistory

# Appendix L
## Youth, the Catholic Church, and Our Future

Full document available in color at:
https://dornsife.usc.edu/iacs/IACShistory

# Appendix M
## 2017 IACS Board Of Trustees

Full document available in color at:
https://dornsife.usc.edu/iacs/IACShistory

**Institute for Advanced Catholic Studies Board of Trustees**
**Fall 2017**

**John Bessolo**

John Bessolo spent the first several years of his career with the Los Angeles office of Price Waterhouse where he became a CPA. From 1985-1993 he worked for Ernst & Young where he was a member of the Entrepreneurial Services Group and a co-director of the Personal Financial Counseling Specialty Group for the Los Angeles area offices. Prior to founding Bessolo Haworth & Vogel LLP, he spent 15 years as a partner at a Los Angeles firm of approximately 120 people. His clients draw on his more than 30 years of experience in financial planning, estate planning and taxation, income taxation and wealth management services. In August 2007, he was recognized by The San Fernando Valley Business Journal as one of the TOP 25 CPA's in the San Fernando Valley. A sought after resource in personal financial planning, Mr. Bessolo has given numerous presentations and has written articles dealing with estate planning concepts and issues affecting owners of privately held businesses.

Mr. Bessolo received his Bachelor's degree in Accounting from the University of Southern California and his Master's degree in Taxation from Golden Gate University. He is a member of the American Institute of Certified Public Accountants and the California Society of Certified Public Accountants. He holds the Personal Financial Specialist (PFS) designation from the AICPA and is a Registered Investment Advisor Representative. Mr. Bessolo is also a licensed life insurance agent.

# Appendix N

## 2023 IACS Board Of Trustees

Available in color at: https://dornsife.usc.edu/iacs/IACShistory

### Appendix N: 2023 IACS Board Members

# BOARD OF TRUSTEES

Institute for Advanced Catholic Studies at USC

The Institute for Advanced Catholic Studies at USC is led by trustees who are leaders in the worlds of business, tech, philanthropy, arts, academia and religion. IACS trustees provide governance and oversight while working collaboratively to further our mission of advancing the exploration of Catholic thought, imagination and experience. IACS trustees also serve as ambassadors, helping communicate the Institute's initiatives, programs and goals within their networks and among the public.

**Kyle Ballarta**
Founder and CEO, Falkon Ventures

**John Bessolo III**
CPA, PFS, Vice Chair of the Board, partner, Eide Bailly LLP

**Thomas J. Condon**
Philanthropist

**Dominic F. Doyle, Ph.D.**
Associate professor of theology, Boston College School of Theology and Ministry

**Rev. Michael Engh, S.J.**
Chancellor, Loyola Marymount University

**Daniel Finn, Ph.D.**
Professor of Theology and Clemens Professor of Economics at St. John's University and the College of St. Benedict

**Rich Grimes**
Managing principal, Tournament Wireless Strategies LLC

**Rev. Bryan Hehir**
Parker Gilbert Montgomery Professor of the Practice of Religion and Public Life, Kennedy School of Government at Harvard University, and Secretariat for Health and Social Services, Archdiocese of Boston

**Rev. Dennis H. Holtschneider, C.M.**
C.M., president, Association of Catholic Colleges and Universities

**Julie McAndrews Mork**
Retired managing director, ECA Foundation, a private, corporate foundation based in Denver with a focus on youth and education.

**Michael P. Moreland, J.D., Ph.D.**
Chair of the Board, University Professor of Law and Religion and Director of the Eleanor H. McCullen Center for Law, Religion and Public Policy at Villanova University

**Patrick Pascal**
President and chief executive officer, Chelsea Management Co.

**Bro. Bernard Ploeger**
Ph.D., assistant provincial for the Marianist Province of the United States.

**Maureen Shea**
CEO and co-founder, Right Management – Florida/Caribbean Region

**Martin J. Skrip**
Retired, KPMG LLP senior corporate tax partner

**Rev. Martin Solma, S.M.**
Chaplain, Chaminade University in Honolulu

**Peter Steinfels**
Retired author, religion columnist for The New York Times, University Professor at Fordham University and Co-Director of the Fordham Center on Religion and Culture

**Jason Zenk**
Senior managing director, EnTrustGlobal

# Works Cited

Adler, Gary J., Jr., ed. *Secularism, Catholicism, and the Future of Public Life: A Dialogue with Ambassador Douglas W. Kmiec*. New York: Oxford University Press, 2015.

Adler, Gary J., Jr., et al., eds. *American Parishes: Remaking Local Catholicism*. New York: Fordham University Press, 2019.

Aquinas, Thomas. *Contra Gentiles: On the Truth of the Catholic Faith*. Edited by Joseph Kenny. New York: Hanover House, 1955-57. https://isidore.co/aquinas/ContraGentiles.htm.

Basinger, Julianne. "Other People's Money." *Chronicle of Higher Education*, Apr. 5, 2002. https://www.chronicle.com/article/other-peoples-money-22032/.

Caulfield, Brian. "Academic Institute to Sidestep Bishops." *National Catholic Register*, Mar. 28, 1999. https://www.ncregister.com/news/academic-institute-to-sidestep-bishops.

Cosgrove, Jim. "Academic Institute Seeks $60 Million." *National Catholic Register*, July 25-31, 1999, 1.

Ellis, John Tracy. "American Catholics and the Intellectual Life." *Thought* 30 (1955) 351-88. https://doi.org/10.5840/thought195530331.

Finn, Daniel K., ed. *Rethinking Justice in Catholic Social Thought*. Washington, DC: Georgetown University Press, 2025.

———. *True Wealth of Nations: Catholic Social Thought and Economic Life*. New York: Oxford University Press, 2010.

Flexner, Abraham. "The Usefulness of Useless Knowledge." *Harpers* (1939) 544-52. https://www.ias.edu/sites/default/files/library/UsefulnessHarpers.pdf.

Gleason, Philip. "What Made Catholic Identity a Problem?" Marianist Award Lecture, University of Dayton, Jan. 27, 1994.

Hayes, Patrick. *A Catholic Brain Trust: The History of the Catholic Commission on Intellectual and Cultural Affairs, 1945-1965*. Notre Dame: University of Notre Dame Press, 2011.

Heft, James L., ed. *Beyond Violence: Religious Sources of Social Transformation in Judaism, Christianity, and Islam*. Abrahamic Dialogues Series 1. New York: Fordham University Press, 2004.

———, ed. *Catholicism and Interreligious Dialogue*. New York: Oxford University Press, 2011.

———, ed. *Faith and the Intellectual Life: Marianist Award Lectures*. Notre Dame: University of Notre Dame Press, 1996.

———. *The Future of Catholic Higher Education: The Open Circle*. New York: Oxford University Press, 2021.

———. "Have Catholic Colleges Reached an Impasse?" *Chronicle of Higher Education* 46 (1999) 89–90.

———, ed. *Passing on the Faith: Transforming Traditions for the Next Generation of Jews, Christians, and Muslims*. Abrahamic Dialogues Series 6. New York: Fordham University Press, 2006.

———. "Tradition: A Catholic Understanding." In *The Idea of Tradition in the Late Modern World: An Ecumenical and Interreligious Conversation*, edited by Thomas Albert Howard, 33–55. Eugene, OR: Cascade, 2020.

Heft, James L., and Jan E. Stets, eds. *Empty Churches: Non-Affiliation in America*. New York: Oxford University Press, 2021.

Heft, James L., et al., eds. *Learned Ignorance: Intellectual Humility Among Jews, Christians, and Muslims*. New York: Oxford University Press, 2011.

Heitmann, John Alfred. "Doing 'True Science': The Early History of the Institutum Divi Thomae: 1935–1951." *Catholic Historical Review* 88 (2002) 702–22. https://dx.doi.org/10.1353/cat.2003.0027.

Hollinger, David A. *Science, Jews, and Secular Culture: Studies in Mid-Twentieth Century American Intellectual History*. Princeton: Princeton University Press, 1998.

Hügel, Friedrich von. "The Three Elements of Religion." In vol. 1 of *The Mystical Element of Religion: As Studied in Saint Catherine of Genoa and Her Friends*, 50–82. London: J. M. Dent & Sons, 1923. https://www.google.com/books/edition/The_Mystical_Element_of_Religion_as_Stud/7OUAAAAAMAAJ?hl=en&gbpv=0.

John Paul II, Pope. "On Catholic Universities" [*Ex Corde Ecclesiae*]. Vatican, Aug. 15, 1990. https://www.vatican.va/content/john-paul-ii/en/apost_constitutions/documents/hf_jp-ii_apc_15081990_ex-corde-ecclesiae.html.

———, propagator. "Title I: The Obligations and Rights of All the Christian Faithful." In *Code of Canon Law*. London: Collins, 1983. https://www.vatican.va/archive/cod-iuris-canonici/eng/documents/cic_lib2-cann208-329_en.html#TITLE_I.

———, propagator. "Title V: Associations of the Christian Faithful." In *Code of Canon Law*. London: Collins, 1983. https://www.vatican.va/archive/cod-iuris-canonici/eng/documents/cic_lib2-cann208-329_en.html#TITLE_V.

Lacey, Michael J. "The Backwardness of American Catholicism." *Proceedings of the Forty-Sixth Annual Convention* 46 (1991) 1–15. https://ejournals.bc.edu/index.php/ctsa/article/view/3604/3196.

Lacey, Michael J., and Francis Oakley, eds. *The Crisis of Authority in Catholic Modernity*. New York: Oxford University Press, 2011.

## Works Cited

Leahy, William P. *Adapting to America: Catholics, Jesuits, and Higher Education in the 20th Century*. Washington, DC: Georgetown University Press, 1991.

Miles, Jack. *God in the Qur'an*. New York: Alfred A. Knopf, 2018.

Mize, Sandra Yocum. *Joining the Revolution in Theology: The College Theology Society, 1954–2004*. Lanham, MD: Rowman & Littlefield, 2007.

Monan, Donald J., and Edward A. Malloy. "*Ex Corde Ecclesiae* Creates an Impasse." *America Magazine* (1999) 6–12.

National Conference of Catholic Bishops. *The Challenge of Peace: God's Promise and Our Response*. Washington, DC: 1983. https://www.usccb.org/upload/challenge-peace-gods-promise-our-response-1983.pdf.

Newman, John Henry. *A Cardinal's Apostolate: October 1881 to December 1884*. Vol. 30 of *The Letters and Diaries of John Henry Newman*, edited by Charles Stephen Dessain. Oxford: Clarendon, 1976.

———. *An Essay in Aid of a Grammar of Assent*. London: Longmans, Green, and Co., 1903. https://www.google.com/books/edition/An_Essay_in_Aid_of_a_Grammar_of_Assent/vb_mWqBm9pMC?hl=en&gbpv=0.

———. *Lectures on the Prophetical Office of the Church, Viewed Relatively to Romanism and Popular Protestantism*. London: Rivington, 1838. https://www.google.com/books/edition/Lectures_on_the_Prophetical_Office_of_th/jFsJAAAAQAAJ?hl=en&gbpv=0.

Noonan, John T., Jr. "An Institute for Advanced Catholic Studies." *America* 183 (2000) 7–11. https://www.americamagazine.org/issue/303/article/institute-advanced-catholic-studies.

Paul VI, Pope. *Apostolicam Actuositatem*. Vatican, Nov. 18, 1965. https://www.vatican.va/archive/hist_councils/ii_vatican_council/documents/vat-ii_decree_19651118_apostolicam-actuositatem_en.html.

———. *Evangelii Nuntiandi*. Vatican, Dec. 8, 1975. https://www.vatican.va/content/paul-vi/en/apost_exhortations/documents/hf_p-vi_exh_19751208_evangelii-nuntiandi.html.

———. "On the Church in the Modern World: *Gaudium Et Spes*." Vatican, Dec. 7, 1965. https://www.vatican.va/archive/hist_councils/ii_vatican_council/documents/vat-ii_const_19651207_gaudium-et-spes_en.html.

Peters, Edward N., curator. "Title 18: On Associations of the Faithful in General." In *1917 or Pio-Benedictine Code of Canon Law, in English Translation*, 241–45. San Francisco: Ignatius, 2001. https://ia801605.us.archive.org/23/items/1917-or-pio-benedictine-code-of-canon/1917%20or%20Pio-Benedictine%20Code%20of%20Canon.pdf.

Pius XI, Pope. "Discourse to Italian Catholic Young Women." *L'Osservatore Romano* (1927) 14.

Prusak, Bernard, and Jennifer Reed-Bouley, eds. *Catholic Higher Education and Catholic Social Thought*. Mahwah, NJ: Paulist, 2023.

Sample, Steven. *The Contrarian's Guide to Leadership*. San Francisco: Jossey-Bass, 2003.

## Works Cited

Schumacher, Mary. "$50 Million Catholic Center to Be Built at National Shrine—Namesake Facility Will Focus on Pope." *Washington Times*, July 23, 1997.

"Something New." *Commonweal* 127 (2000) 5–6. https://www.commonwealmagazine.org/something-new.

Taylor, Charles. *The Varieties of Religion Today*. Cambridge: Harvard University Press, 2002.

Weigel, Gustave. "Gustave Weigel, S.J. (1906–1964)." CatholicAuthors.com. http://www.catholicauthors.com/weigel.html.

# Index

Academic Advisory Council, 34, 36–37, 39, 55, 109, 112
Adler, Gary J., 81–83, 99
American Catholic Historical Association, 4
American Catholic Sociological Association, 4
Anderson, William, xix-xx
Appleby, Scott, 14, 20, 25, 60, 89
Argidius Foundation, 16, 61
Aymond, Gregory, 46
Aquinas, Thomas. *See* Thomas Aquinas.
Association of Catholic Colleges and Universities (ACCU), 4, 19, 47
Association of Graduate Deans of Catholic Universities, xx

Baker, Jack, 103
Bamberger, Louis, 1, 79
Benedict XVI, 58n, 82, 90. *See* Josef Ratzinger.
Bessolo, John, 89–90
Buckley, Michael, 41
Burrell, David, 71

Caron, Paul, 20, 33–34, 56, 63, 69–71
Catholic Action movement, 7

Catholic Commission on Intellectual and Cultural Affairs (CCICA), 5–6, 8–16
Catholic Intellectual Tradition, ix-xi, 15, 18, 41, 60, 70, 88, 92–96, 106–7
Center for Advanced Study in the Behavioral Sciences, 16
Cerling, Becky, 99
*Challenge of Peace*, 96
Chaminade University, 86, 89
Code of Canon Law (1917), 9
Code of Canon Law (1983), 22
Coleman, John, 28, 102
Commission on Catholic Scholarship (CCS), xv, 20–21, 25, 30–33, 43, 60–61, 111
Condon, Tom, 28, 98
Conway, Jill Ker, 23, 56, 67, 69, 73
Cottier, Georges, xvi, 55–56

Danneels, Godfried Maria Jules, 25–26, 60
Dayton, University of, xv-xvi, xix, 1, 3, 6, 14, 17, 29, 51–52, 65, 73–75, 79, 86, 105
DePaul University, 87
Downey, Michael, 50
Doyle, Dominic F., 90
Duffy, James, 34

elevator speech, 24, 92–93, 96, 122

## Index

Ellis, John Tracy, 6–7, 12, 15
Erasmus Institute, 41–43, 80
*Ex Corde Ecclesiae*, x, 14, 46–49
Euart, Sharon, 22

Finn, Daniel K., 71, 102
Firestone, Reuven, 72–73, 100, 123
Fitz, Raymond L., 17, 105
Flexner, Abraham, 1–3, 13, 24, 106, 127
Føllesdal, Dagfinn, 35, 38
Fuld, Mrs. Felix, 1
fundraising, 26, 33, 52–54, 56–57, 59–76, 79–80, 88–89, 91, 96

Garrett, Elizabeth, 83–84, 83n, 98
Garrison, Sheila, xvi, 83
Generations in Dialogue (GID), 81–82, 88–89, 102–3, 120
Georgetown University, 4, 20 43–45, 66
Gioia, Dana, 82–83
Gleason, Philip, 6, 15, 43
Glodeck, Stephen, 54
Gold, Stanley, 87
Gomez, José, 57, 80, 102

Hancock, Ellen, 23, 73, 90
Hayes, Patrick, 8–11, 13–14
Hehir, J. Bryan, 67
Herscher, Uri, 87
Hesburgh, Theodore, xxi
Holtschneider, Dennis H., 87
Hügel, Friedrich von, 95
Hussain, Amir, 100, 123
Hutchins, Robert M., 7

*Institutum Divi Thomae* (IDT), 5, 15
Institute for Advanced Study, 1, 13, 16, 23, 34, 106
interreligious dialogue, 13, 36, 39, 72, 91–92, 101

Jesuit Institute, 41–43

John Paul II, 14, 22–23, 40–41, 46, 48, 55, 58
John Paul II Cultural Center, Pope, 40–41

Kaveny, Cathleen, 35
Keightley, Georgia, 32
Komonchak, Joseph, 21n, 38
Kreditor, Alan, 75, 98

Lacey, Michael, xv, 17–20, 28, 33–34, 38, 40, 42–43, 63, 70
Lamb, Matthew, 47, 50
Law, Bernard, 50–52, 55
Leahy, William P., 44
Lipscomb, Oscar, 38–39
localism, x, 16, 18, 33, 43–44, 59–61, 74, 86–87
Longley, Clifford, 70–71
Lumen Christi Institute, 43

McElroy, Robert W., ix–xi
McGinn, Bernard, 35, 88
Mahony, Roger, 50–58, 80
Marianists (Society of Mary), xv, 54, 75, 83–84
Martini, Carlo Maria, 25–26, 60
Miller, Amber, 98
Miller, Donald, 72
Mork, Julie and John, 83
Murray, John Courtney, 9, 12

National Catholic Educational Association (NCEA), 9, 33, 46
National Catholic Welfare Council, 9
National Humanities Center, 16
Newman, John Henry, 94–95
Nikias, Max, 80, 82–83, 89, 98
Noonan, John, 20, 27–28, 34, 49, 114
Novak, Michael, 35, 38
Notre Dame Institute for Advanced Study, 80, 85

O'Brien, David, 14–15, 20

## Index

O'Brien, John A., 9
O'Malley, John, 82
Oakley, Francis, 34, 56, 69–70
Örsy, Ladislas, 22

Paul VI, 23, 94
Paulraj, Arogyaswami, 34
Pilarczyk, Daniel, 35, 38–39, 49–51, 115
Pings, Cornelius (Neal), 28, 98
Pius XI, 7–8
Ploeger, Bernard J., xvi, 89
Portier, William, xvi
Princeton University, 1–2, 6, 13, 16, 23, 26, 34, 65, 69, 79, 103, 106

Ratzinger, Josef, xvi, 51, 115–18. *See* Benedict XVI.
Roche, Mark, xvi
Rooney, William J., 11–12
Roski, Ed, 103
Rossi, Ernesto, 55–56

St. Mary's University, San Antonio, 86
Sample, Steven, 28–30, 69, 80, 83, 87, 91, 97–98

Second Vatican Council. *See* Vatican Council II.
Shea, Maureen, 83
Shuster, George, 9
Signer, Michael, 71
Solma, Martin, 83, 90
Stanford, Edward, 11–12
Starr, Kevin, 28, 34, 98
Stets, Jan, xvi, 101

Taylor, Charles, 20, 35, 38
Templeton Foundation, 66
Thomas Aquinas, 8, 38, 102
Turner, James, 41

Valkenburg, Wilhelmus (Pim), 100, 123
Vatican Council II, xiii, xvi, 3, 8, 10–13, 22, 91, 94–95
Vincentians, 74, 79, 87, 103

Wolfe, Gregory, 88
Wood, Richard, xvi
Woodrow Wilson Center, 16–17, 34

Yale University, 17, 26, 76